IEA Research for Educators

Evidence-based and Instructional Materials for Teachers Using Data from the International Association for the Evaluation of Educational Achievement (IEA)

Volume 1

The International Association for the Evaluation of Educational Achievement (IEA) is an independent nongovernmental nonprofit cooperative of national research institutions and governmental research agencies that originated in Hamburg, Germany in 1958. For over 60 years, IEA has developed and conducted high-quality, large-scale comparative studies in education to support countries' efforts to engage in national strategies for educational monitoring and improvement.

IEA continues to promote capacity building and knowledge sharing to foster innovation and quality in education, proudly uniting more than 60 member institutions, with studies conducted in more than 100 countries worldwide.

IEA's comprehensive data provide an unparalleled longitudinal resource for researchers and educators. The founders of IEA viewed the world as a natural educational laboratory, where different school systems experiment in different ways to obtain optimal results from educating their youth. They assumed that if research could obtain evidence from across a wide range of systems, the variability would be sufficient to reveal important relationships that would otherwise escape detection within a single education system. They strongly rejected data-free assertions about the relative merits of various education systems and aimed to identify factors that would have meaningful and consistent influences on educational outcomes.

In line with this, this series of peer-reviewed publications is established to contribute to educational practices. The goal is to inspire educators by translating IEA research findings into evidence-based practice, and to foster engagement and conversation between researchers and practitioners.

More information about this series at https://link.springer.com/bookseries/16856

Marian Bruggink · Nicole Swart ·
Annelies van der Lee · Eliane Segers

Putting PIRLS to Use in Classrooms Across the Globe

Evidence-Based Contributions for Teaching Reading Comprehension in a Multilingual Context

 Springer

Marian Bruggink
Dutch Center for Language Education
(Expertisecentrum Nederlands)
Nijmegen, The Netherlands

Nicole Swart
Dutch Center for Language Education
(Expertisecentrum Nederlands)
Nijmegen, The Netherlands

Annelies van der Lee
Dutch Center for Language Education
(Expertisecentrum Nederlands)
Nijmegen, The Netherlands

Eliane Segers
Dutch Center for Language Education
(Expertisecentrum Nederlands)
Nijmegen, The Netherlands

ISSN 2731-4979   ISSN 2731-4987 (electronic)
IEA Research for Educators
ISBN 978-3-030-95265-5   ISBN 978-3-030-95266-2   (eBook)
https://doi.org/10.1007/978-3-030-95266-2

This Springer imprint is published by the registered company Springer Nature Switzerland AG
The registered company address is: Gewerbestrasse 11, 6330 Cham, Switzerland

Series Editors' Foreword

IEA's mission is to enhance knowledge about education systems worldwide and to provide high-quality data that will support education reform and lead to better teaching and learning in schools. In pursuit of this aim, it conducts, and reports on, major studies of student achievement in literacy, mathematics, science, citizenship, and digital literacy. These studies, notably PIRLS, TIMSS, ICCS, and ICILS, are well established and have set the benchmark for international comparative studies in education.

The studies have generated vast datasets encompassing student achievement, disaggregated in a variety of ways, along with a wealth of contextual information which contains considerable explanatory power. The numerous reports that have emerged from them are a valuable contribution to the corpus of educational research.

Valuable though these detailed reports are, IEA's goal of supporting education reform needs something more: deep understanding of education systems and the many factors that bear on student learning advances through in-depth analysis of the global datasets. IEA has long championed such analysis and facilitates scholars and policymakers in conducting secondary analysis of our datasets. So, we provide software such as the International Database Analyzer to encourage the analysis of our datasets and support numerous publications including a peer-reviewed journal, *Large-scale Assessments in Education*, our policy brief series, IEA Compass: Briefs in Education, and our IEA Research for Education book series providing a powerful information avenue for researchers and policymakers. We also organize a biennial international research conference to nurture exchanges between researchers and policymakers working with IEA data.

The **IEA Research for Educators** series represents an exciting effort by IEA to capitalize on our datasets for a new audience, teachers. IEA studies have always been a great resource for researchers and policymakers. However, the desire remained to give something back to those schools and teachers who responded to studies and provided the valuable information that is gathered and organized in the form of an international database.

Because IEA studies' design and instruments target the system level, not a classroom or individual one, since the beginning of our studies there have been discussions around how best to engage with and provide helpful information to teachers.

Our aim is to connect the growing body of knowledge based on IEA studies, as well as other research findings, with school and classroom realities. This series aims to translate IEA study data into evidence-based and instructional materials for teachers and, in doing so, foster engagement and conversation between researchers and practitioners.

This book is the first volume in this newly developed series and focuses on the translation of PIRLS data to practical information for teaching reading comprehension. PIRLS, the Progress in International Reading Literacy Study, is one of the core studies of IEA and provides trends and international comparisons of fourth grade students' reading literacy achievement and associated factors. Directed by the TIMSS and PIRLS International Study Center at Boston College and conducted every five years since 2001, PIRLS is recognized as the global standard for assessing trends in reading achievement at the fourth grade.

PIRLS assesses the two overarching purposes for reading that account for most of the reading done by young students both in and out of school: for literary experience and to acquire and use information. In addition, PIRLS assesses four broad-based comprehension processes within each of the two purposes for reading: focus on and retrieve explicitly stated information, make straightforward inferences, interpret and integrate ideas and information, and evaluate and critique content and textual elements. In addition to reading assessment, the PIRLS school, teacher, student, and home questionnaires gather extensive information about the contextual factors at home and school which are associated with the teaching and learning of reading. These rich data include information on how the education system is organized to facilitate learning; students' home environment and supports for learning; school climate and resources, and how instruction usually occurs in the classroom. PIRLS also provides an encyclopedia that includes data about each country's educational context for learning to read.

As said, the PIRLS target population are fourth grade students, PIRLS has chosen this grade because these students are making the transition from *learning to read* to *reading to learn*. For each PIRLS assessment, a representative sample of students from each participating country are selected. Schools are selected at random, but in a systematic manner, using a carefully designed sampling frame by independent IEA experts. In most countries, 150 schools are selected to participate in PIRLS, representing 4000 students, although this differs between countries. Using a sampling frame composed of all eligible schools ensures that all different types of schools are represented in the sample. For example, the size of the school is considered to ensure that students from both large and small schools are selected, as well as schools from big cities and small villages. Our careful procedures make sure that the sample will give a true and complete picture of the target grade students in a country, and that these "pictures" are comparable between countries.

The PIRLS data utilized in this volume provides an overview of the current insights and literature on reading comprehension, while PIRLS passages and items assist to provide practical illustrations of the reading processes and didactic suggestions discussed. The book is divided into two parts. In the first part of this book, the authors describe the major theories regarding reading comprehension and give an overview of recent scientific insights. Factors that influence the development of students' reading comprehension skills are then discussed with an eye on individual variation. Evidence-based didactic principles in reading comprehension and practical teaching suggestions are illustrated with example lessons to assist to outline how teachers can support their students in reading comprehension. A review of two PIRLS texts and question items concretize the reading processes outlined.

In the second part, the book has a specific focus on teaching reading to multilingual students, a topic relevant for many teachers around the world. Scientific insights regarding reading education for multilingual students are described, followed by guidelines and examples on how to use these in day-to-day practice. Additionally, good practices from seven schools in five participating PIRLS countries are described. Teachers from these schools present how they and their schools work on reading comprehension, specifically for multilingual students, with practical tips and tools and example lessons. These insights into daily reading education in multilingual classrooms can be an inspiration to teachers all over the world.

From inception it was recognized that in order to achieve the aims of this series, IEA would need to tap into the skillset and experience of its member institutions, national research centers, and other partners involved in IEA studies. This additional expertise would allow us to create a bridge between the available resources, classroom contexts, and those who can appreciate and use them, teachers. We are extremely grateful to the team of authors from Expertisecentrum Nederlands, an institution that has been the national study center for PIRLS in the Netherlands since 2001, for their dedication to the development of the first volume in this new series and new IEA format. This book will be a valuable resource for teachers and teacher educators, and we look forward to continuing this book series and work together with experts who can bridge the research world and the classroom practice.

Andrea Netten
Paulína Koršňáková
Series Editors

Preface

A good understanding of written texts is an essential skill in the literate society we live in. Well-developed reading comprehension skills are not only required for learning and acquiring new knowledge, but also required for day-to-day activities. Helping students to develop their reading comprehension skills is, therefore, one of the core and most complicated tasks for teachers all over the world. Reading comprehension is a complex skill, mainly taking place in the mind of the reader. Over the past decades, numerous scientific studies have examined how readers come to understand written texts and how teachers can aid students in developing these comprehension skills. Although a lot is known and information on how to teach reading comprehension skills is available, this knowledge does not always transfer to classroom practice.

In this book, we aim to bridge the gap between science and practice and help teachers transform the latest scientific insights regarding reading comprehension into didactic guidelines to use in everyday practice for all students. This book consists of two parts. Part I, *Reading Comprehension: From Research to Practical Teaching Guidelines*, comprises three chapters and discusses the teaching of reading comprehension in general. In Chapter 1 we briefly describe some of the most prominent theories of reading comprehension and create a solid base for the rest of the book. Chapter 1 serves as an introduction to the evidence-based didactic principles presented in Chapter 2, that can be used to help children develop their reading comprehension skills. In Chapter 3, two PIRLS texts are used to show how teachers and other educational professionals can use the PIRLS results in order to determine which reading processes need more attention in their classrooms and how these can be taught using the didactic principles presented in Chapter 2.

In Part II, *Teaching Reading Comprehension in a Multilingual Classroom*, we focus on multilingual students. Almost all teachers deal with multilingual students in their classrooms and therefore face additional challenges as there is already a large variation in reading comprehension skills within their classroom. However, multilingualism also has many advantages. Recognizing and using the home languages of multilingual children at school can have a positive impact on their well-being, self-confidence, and identity development. Children who grow up at home with the same language used at school also benefit from integrating multilingualism in education.

They develop language awareness and a positive attitude toward other languages and cultures. Chapter 4 describes the theoretical insights on reading comprehension and multilingualism and the specific principles that apply to teaching this group of students. Finally, in Chapter 5, we describe the responses from teachers in five PIRLS countries across the globe who responded to our request for insights into the daily reading education in their multilingual classroom. With this book, we hope to inspire teachers to reflect on their current reading comprehension lessons and further base their lessons on evidence-based insights, so that they can prepare their students to become the best possible readers with an enthusiasm for reading.

Nijmegen, The Netherlands   Marian Bruggink
                                                                             Nicole Swart
                                                                        Annelies van der Lee
                                                                             Eliane Segers
                                                                                 Authors

Acknowledgments The authors would like to thank our helpful contributors for their input and feedback. Thank you to Hedi Kwakkel, Martine Hagen, and Merel Vriens for your feedback on Chapters 1–4. Chapter 5 could not have been written without the good practices shared from schools around the world. We would like to thank the schools, teachers, and national research coordinators (NRCs) who have contributed to the realization of these good practices. We would also like to thank the IEA's Publications and Editorial Committee for their invaluable contributions, which enhanced the overall quality of this book.

Contents

About the Authors

Drs. Marian Bruggink has a master's degree in Education and also worked as a primary school teacher. She started working at the Dutch Center for Language Education in 2001. Besides the PIRLS project, she participated in many other language and reading projects. She mainly develops educational guidelines and teaching materials for language education, based on scientific research.

Dr. Nicole Swart started working at the Dutch Center for Language Education in 2017 after completing her Ph.D. at the Radboud University on the role of vocabulary in reading comprehension in the upper primary grades. Since then she has participated in various reading comprehension oriented research projects, including PIRLS-2021.

Annelies van der Lee, M.A. finished her master's degree in Linguistics at Radboud University in Nijmegen in 2018 and has been working at the Dutch Center for Language Education since then. She has contributed to various projects concerning second language acquisition and education, including a national pilot in bilingual primary education, and is also part of the PIRLS team.

Prof. Dr. Eliane Segers has a chair in Learning and Technology at Radboud University, and a chair (via the Reading Foundation) on Reading and Digital Media at the University of Twente. She is Scientific Director of the Dutch Center for Language Education, and has conducted several research projects regarding reading comprehension in both monolingual and bilingual students (see https://scholar.google.com/citations?hl=nl&user=SSgyX1MAAAAJ), and is the Senior Researcher in the current Dutch PIRLS project.

Part I
Reading Comprehension: From Research to Practical Teaching Guidelines

Chapter 1
Theories of Reading Comprehension

The Current State of Affairs on Reading Comprehension Research

Abstract This chapter aims to provide teachers with a brief overview of the current state of affairs in reading comprehension research, serving as a frame of reference and support for the rest of the book. Comprehending a written text requires the reader to identify the words used in the text, combine single word meanings into propositions, and subsequently create a coherent and adequate model of the text. Together with relevant background knowledge, a shallow textbase can be enhanced into a more in-depth situation model which depicts the situation described in the text. There are a number of factors that have proven to have an impact on how well a reader understands a text, such as word identification abilities, language comprehension abilities, the use of reading comprehension strategies, and reading motivation. Also in this chapter, the various purposes of reading and processes for comprehension as described in the PIRLS assessment framework are explained.

Keywords Reading comprehension · Text model · Reading factors · Reading purposes · Comprehension processes · Progress in International Reading Literacy Study (PIRLS)

1.1 Introduction

Reading comprehension is a crucial skill in modern-day society. Readers lacking comprehension skills face challenges in everyday life, from understanding a medicine's package insert to dealing with online information, and acquiring new knowledge. But what does it mean to comprehend a text? What does it take for the reader to arrive at comprehension? This chapter aims to provide teachers with a brief overview of the current state of affairs in reading comprehension research, serving as a frame of reference and support for the rest of this book. At the end of this chapter, reading tips are provided for those who are interested in learning more about theories of reading comprehension and reading comprehension research.

M. Bruggink et al., *Putting PIRLS to Use in Classrooms Across the Globe*, IEA Research for Educators 1, https://doi.org/10.1007/978-3-030-95266-2_1

In accordance with recent comprehension models and the Progress in International Reading Literacy Study (PIRLS) framework, reading literacy can be defined as:

> the ability to use and understand those written language formats required by society and/or valued by the individual. Readers can construct meaning from written texts in a variety of forms. They read to learn, to participate in communities of readers in school and everyday life, and for enjoyment (Mullis & Martin, 2019, p. 6).

This definition of reading comprehension reflects various theories in which reading comprehension is seen as a constructive and interactive process. It is the product of the interaction between factors at both the level of the reader and the text (Kintsch, 1998; Perfetti & Stafura, 2014; Van den Broek et al., 1999). Reading comprehension, therefore, requires a broad set of skills and a certain level of prior knowledge on the part of the reader. In addition, the present definition also reflects three overarching purposes for reading, namely, reading for pleasure and personal interest, learning, and participation in society. Young readers' reading is mainly centered around the first two reading purposes. Therefore, the PIRLS assessment framework is focused around these two, using narrative texts to assess literary experience (pleasure and personal interest) and informative texts to assess the acquisition and use of information (learning).

Regardless of the purpose of reading, comprehension ideally results in an adequate and representative model of the text. According to the construction-integration model of reading comprehension, texts are represented at three levels: the surface structure, the textbase, and the situation model (Kintsch, 1998). The *surface structure* consists of the words in the text and the ideas that these words represent. The ideas are referred to as propositions and reflect what is explicitly stated in the text (i.e., facts, events, feelings, etc.). The *textbase* is created by connecting the single propositions and "represents the meaning of the text, as it is actually expressed by the text" (Kintsch & Rawson, 2005, p. 211). Although the textbase provides the reader with information stated in the text, comprehension will be shallow since the reader understands only what is explicitly stated in the text. For a deeper understanding, the reader has to create a model of the situation. Creating such a *situation model* requires the integration of both information explicitly stated in the text (i.e., the textbase) and relevant prior/background knowledge.

Textbox 1.1: The difference between a textbase and a situation model

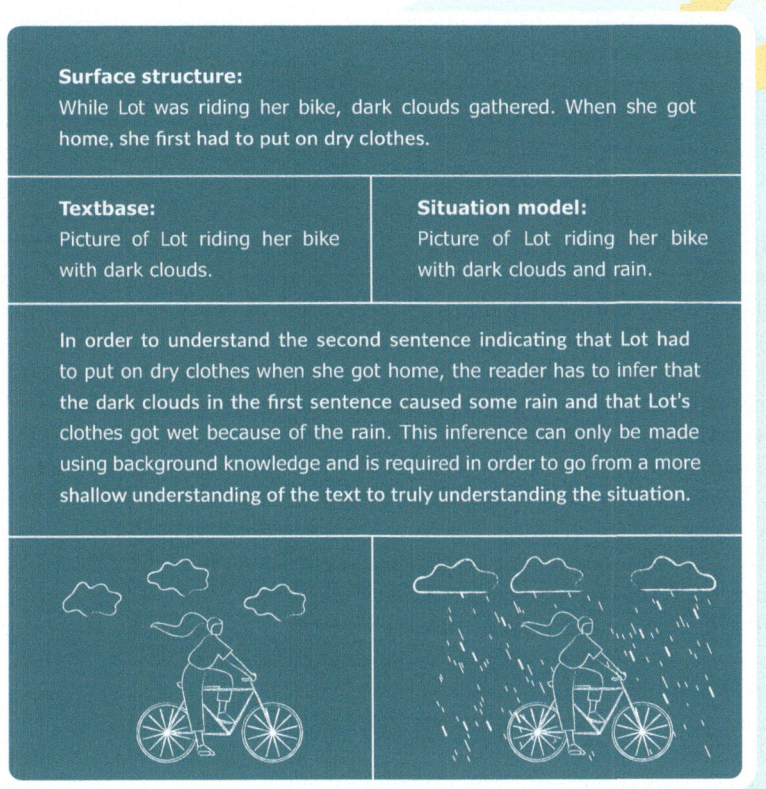

Surface structure:
While Lot was riding her bike, dark clouds gathered. When she got home, she first had to put on dry clothes.

Textbase:	**Situation model:**
Picture of Lot riding her bike with dark clouds.	Picture of Lot riding her bike with dark clouds and rain.

In order to understand the second sentence indicating that Lot had to put on dry clothes when she got home, the reader has to infer that the dark clouds in the first sentence caused some rain and that Lot's clothes got wet because of the rain. This inference can only be made using background knowledge and is required in order to go from a more shallow understanding of the text to truly understanding the situation.

1.2   What Does it Take to Comprehend a Text?

Understanding a written text is a complex process and in order to recognize what it takes to comprehend a text, it is important to know how readers construct meaning from a text. According to the Simple View of Reading (SVR) model (Gough & Tunmer, 1986), reading comprehension involves two main skills: being able to identify the words in a text by converting letters into sounds and combining these into words (i.e., decoding) and the ability to comprehend orally presented information (i.e., language comprehension). The SVR model states that comprehension is not merely the sum of both decoding and language comprehension skills, but that it can be seen as the product of it: reading comprehension = decoding x language comprehension, with scores for decoding and language comprehension ranging between 0 and 1. This formula indicates that to become a reader with strong comprehension, both skills need to be developed; when one falls behind, the other skill can compensate a little, but the reader will never become a strong reader with strong comprehension ($0.1 \times 1 = 0.1$ and $1 \times 0.1 = 0.1$). So, in order to become a good reader, both skills need to be addressed in school. However, as both skills can be divided again into many subskills (Scarborough, 2001), this is not an easy task.

Although numerous studies support the SVR model, it has been suggested that it is limited in the role it awards to language-specific factors, such as word knowledge (i.e., vocabulary), and that it does not do justice to the complexity of the reading comprehension process. To understand the complex process, a more general framework highlighting various factors is necessary. The Reading Systems Framework (RSF) (Perfetti & Stafura, 2014), is such a framework. According to the RSF, comprehension requires two main subprocesses: word identification and word-to-text integration. Word identification refers to the process of converting letters into sounds, combining these sounds into words, and assigning meaning to the words being read. Activated word meanings, which are stored in the mental lexicon (see Textbox 1.2), are not only seen as the output for word identification, they also function as the input for word-to-text integration. Words that are just activated have to be integrated in order to form a representation of the text. This is referred to as word-to-text integration. In other words, from single words, readers create sentences by integrating single word meanings, which in turn can be combined into a text model (i.e., textbase) and finally a situation model can be constructed. Finally, the RSF places a great deal of importance on incorporating relevant background knowledge to go from a more shallow textbase or text model to a more in-depth situation model. Here, background knowledge does not only refer to knowledge about the subject of the text, but also to knowledge about text structures, text genres, purposes for reading, and the use of reading comprehension strategies. One important aspect that is not covered in the RSF is motivation. It has been suggested that motivation plays a crucial role in becoming a good comprehender (Toste et al., 2020).

In the remainder of this chapter, the role of word identification, word-to-text integration, use of comprehension strategies, and motivation in supporting comprehension of written texts will be discussed in more detail. We have listed a few reading tips at the end of this chapter for teachers who are interested in reading more on the role of these four factors or who want to learn more about the impact of other factors on reading comprehension.

1.2.1 Word Identification

In order to become successful in comprehension, the reader has to develop fluent word identification skills. This is necessary, as all cognitive processes needed to comprehend a written text require part of the reader's limited cognitive resources. To ensure that enough cognitive resources remain available for the comprehension processes, it is important that word identification becomes automatic and does not require too much effort from the reader. Word identification, as the term suggests, is the ability to identify words and consists of two steps: decoding and retrieving semantic information from long-term memory. Word identification starts with decoding, the process of converting strings of letters (orthographic units, known as grapheme) into their corresponding sounds (phonological units, known as phoneme). Becoming a fluent decoder generally is a matter of "practice makes perfect." When children are still learning to crack the code, decoding is a slow and effortful process. Each grapheme has to be consciously converted into its corresponding phoneme, and these phonemes need to be combined into single words. However, the more children practice, the more automatic these actions become. During the primary school years, children rapidly become faster readers (Verhoeven et al., 2011), a process that continues well into adolescence. For most readers, decoding becomes a fast and effortless process, as relating sounds to letters takes less effort as more and more words are (partly) recognized on sight. The ease with which decoding becomes a fast and effortless process partly depends on the language in which students learn to read, and specifically on the transparency of the language (Patel et al., 2004). Transparency of a language has to do with the consistency with which letters correspond to sounds. A language is said to be transparent when consistency between written letters and sounds is high and single letters generally correspond to a single sound, making it easy to convert a string of letters into a word. Examples of transparent languages are Italian, Spanish, and Indonesian. A language is said to be opaque when consistency between written letters and sounds is low and single letters can correspond to more than one sound. An example of a very opaque language is English. Languages such as French, Persian, and Dutch are in the middle. Research has shown that it is easier to learn how to decode words in transparent languages compared to more opaque languages (Patel et al., 2004).

Textbox 1.2: An explanation and illustrating example of the mental lexicon

The mental lexicon is the place in long-term memory where word knowledge is stored. For each known word a lexical representation is created and within this representation orthographic (how a word is written), phonological (how a word is pronounced), and semantic (what a word means) information is stored. The mental lexicon can be compared to a web of interconnected elements in which each lexical representation represents a single node and these nodes are connected with each other. When a single word is activated, for instance because it has been read, other related words are also activated. Using the example in Textbox 1.1. the picture below is of a network around the word "cloud". Notice the related words "rain" and "water," which are crucial in understanding the example in Textbox 1.1. When a reader has not established the relationship between cloud and rain, it is hard or probably even impossible to truly understand the example in Textbox 1.1.

As noted before, word identification is more than being able to decode words; it also includes retrieving semantic information from long-term memory. In other words, after a word has been decoded, information about the meaning of that word becomes activated and the reader can use it to create an understanding of the text. The difference between word identification and its subprocess of decoding can best be illustrated by the following example. An experienced reader is able to easily decode the pseudoword (i.e., nonword) "stremkra." They can convert the orthographic representation (i.e., the written form) into a phonological one (i.e., how it is pronounced). However, while decoding it, no semantic information can be retrieved, since it is not a real word. So, although decoding is possible, identification is not. For the word "rabbit" the situation is different. For most readers, it is easy to identify. Not only do they know how to read the word rabbit, they are also able to retrieve its meaning. In other words, most readers know how to decode it and know what a rabbit looks like, where they live, what colors they can have, that they are usually fluffy, etc.

Word identification is influenced by how well a reader knows a word. For each known word, a lexical representation is stored in the readers' mental lexicon containing information about its written form (orthography), pronunciation (phonology), and meaning (semantics). The quality of these representations depends on how well you know the written form of a word, know how to pronounce it, and know what it means. Researchers refer to this as lexical quality (Perfetti, 2007). Lexical quality varies largely between children: some children know more words and know more about these words than others. Lexical quality also varies within children: some words are easier to spell, pronounce, and understand (i.e., table) as compared to others (i.e., bureaucracy). Low lexical quality is a main cause of poor comprehension. Not only is decoding easier when the reader has access to well-specified lexical representations in terms of how words are written, how they are pronounced, and what they mean (Dyson et al., 2017), but research has also shown that in order to understand a text, the reader has to know the meaning of at least 90–95% of the words in a text (Nagy & Scott, 2000).

1.2.2 Word-to-Text Integration

To comprehend a text, in addition to the ability to read it, the reader has to integrate the individual word meanings into a sentence representation and combine all sentences into a mental model of the text. In other words, in addition to word identification, the comprehension process entails integrating single word meanings into propositions which in turn can be used in order to create the textbase and situation models. This is referred to as word-to-text integration. Combining single words into accurate propositions is crucial in understanding the text: *the man chases the dog* is different from *the dog chases the man*. Although the same five words are used, the meaning of the sentence and, therefore, the meaning of the textbase is completely different. The development of language comprehension skills and integration skills more specifically, starts early on, long before children start to learn to read and identify words. As early as preschool and kindergarten, children develop language skills, such as the ability to generate and memorize sentences and use their vocabulary knowledge, factors that both predict initial reading comprehension ability and its growth (Hjetland et al., 2019).

Textbox 1.3: Examples of how propositions can be related

Repetition of words	Linda and Kai were playing with _the ball_ close to the river, when _the ball_ fell in the water. _The ball_ was quite wet.
Establishing of anaphoric relations	Linda and Kai were playing with _the ball_ close to the river, when _it_ fell in the water and _it_ was quite wet.
Generating other inferences	Linda and Kai were playing with the ball close to the river when the ball fell and was quite wet. (The reader has to infer that the ball fell into the water and therefore was quite wet.)

In comprehending a text, it is not only important to create and understand propositions, but the different propositions also have to be brought together. Just as with creating propositions, combining propositions is a delicate process in which the reader needs to understand the interrelations between two or more pieces of information. There are various ways in which propositions can be related, for example, by the repetition of words, through establishing anaphoric relations, and by generating other types of inferences (see Textbox 1.3).

As indicated above, together these propositions form the textbase. With inclusion of the reader's own relevant prior knowledge but also by using knowledge on text structures, text genres, and the use of comprehension strategies (see Sect. 1.2.3), the reader is able to generate a model of the situation described in the text: the situation model. Relevant background knowledge is thus a crucial part of reading comprehension.

The complete process of creating propositions and combining them into an adequate model of the text can be referred to as word-to-text integration, and readers vary in how these integration skills are developed. One major impacting factor is lexical quality (Perfetti, 2007). Just as with word identification, the amount and quality of word knowledge (written form, pronunciation, and meaning) stored in the mental lexicon has an impact on the ease with which a reader can create a model of the text and the quality of the model. During the integration process, information about the meaning of the word from the semantic constituent is used to connect a word or sentence to the text model created up to that point. Readers with many high-quality lexical representations are able to activate more semantic knowledge, assigning the correct meaning given the context in which the word is used, making it easier to create propositions and combine these into a model of the text. Semantic information, in particular, can aid this integration process. The more semantic information available, the easier it is to create accurate propositions and integrate these propositions into the model of the text.

In addition to individual variations in word-to-text integration abilities, due to differences in lexical quality, variations in texts may have an impact on how easy it is to create a model of the text. Cohesion and genre are two relevant textual factors (McNamara et al., 2011). Text cohesion refers to the degree in which a text provides explicit cues to help the reader relate information from the text. Texts with low cohesion require a lot of inferences from the reader, while highly cohesive texts do not. The latter are thus easier to comprehend. Similarly, readers find it easier to make inferences in narrative texts, as they describe topics that the reader has prior knowledge of (e.g., friendship). Results from a recent meta- analysis confirm that readers generate more inferences during narrative reading as compared to reading expository texts (Clinton et al., 2020). When it is easier to generate inferences, it is easier to create a textbase and situation model and consequently demonstrate understanding of the text.

1.2.3   Comprehension Strategies

A reading strategy can be seen as a "mental tool" that readers can use to support, monitor, and restore their understanding of the text (Afflerbach & Cho, 2009). Readers with strong comprehension skills can be characterized as strategic readers, who both consciously and unconsciously use specific strategies to solve comprehension difficulties and regulate their own reading behavior. Strategies can be divided into cognitive comprehension strategies and metacognitive comprehension strategies.

Cognitive comprehension strategies help the reader to create a coherent and adequate situation model of the text and therefore directly enhance comprehension. These mental tools aid the reader in understanding what they have read by either performing activities before, during, or after reading. Examples of effective cognitive comprehension strategies are: making predictions (before reading), asking questions (during reading), and visualizing the content of the text (after reading). *Metacognitive comprehension strategies* are used to monitor and evaluate whether the constructed mental model (the situation model) is accurate and fits the reading purpose. Examples of effective metacognitive comprehension strategies are: setting reading goals (before reading), monitoring of understanding (during reading), and clarifying of uncertainties (after reading).

Both types of strategies, cognitive and metacognitive, work in conjunction with each other. When a reader, for instance, signals that they do not understand what has just been read (metacognitive comprehension), the reader can ask themselves questions concerning the text (cognitive comprehension) in order to enhance comprehension of that part of the text. Successful readers are able to regulate their use of cognitive and metacognitive reading strategies (Andreassen et al., 2017). The most effective comprehension strategies are further discussed in Sect. 2.2.3.

So far, it has been shown that according to a more interactive model of reading comprehension, RSF, two main subprocesses are in play: (1) word identification where orthographic, phonological, and semantic knowledge is important and activated word meanings are the outcome, and (2) word-to-text integration where these activated word meanings are integrated into sentences, a textbase, and, together with relevant background knowledge, a situation model. A schematic representation of the RSF is presented in Fig. 1.1.

1.2.4 Motivation

Grade 4 has been associated with a so-called "fourth-grade slump" (Chall & Jacobs, 2003). Around this grade, children gradually progress from *learning to read* to *reading to learn* and this is one of the reasons why it is so interesting and important to examine children's reading comprehension skills in grade 4 as is the case with PIRLS. The slump itself refers to the stagnation in growth in reading comprehension starting in fourth grade as children transition from "learning to read" to "reading to learn", and is especially prominent in children with a lower social-economic background (Chall & Jacobs, 2003). Less extensive vocabulary seems to partially cause these problems. Additionally, children with poorer comprehension also tend to lose their motivation to read, thus entering a negative, downward spiral in reading comprehension. An upward spiral of causality has also been documented: more proficient readers are more motivated to read, read more, and further improve their skills (Mol & Bus, 2011).

A meta-study has shown that the nature of the relation between reading skills and motivation is indeed bidirectional (Toste et al., 2020), indicating that not only does motivation have an impact on the ability to comprehend a written text, but that comprehension skills also have an impact on motivation to read. In other words, well-developed comprehension skills boost children's motivation to read and children with more motivation read more frequently, with more pleasure, and develop better reading comprehension skills. The opposite is also true; children with comprehension difficulties are often less motivated to read and therefore read less and have fewer opportunities to develop their comprehension skills, resulting in less-developed skills. However, overall, the conclusion is that success is more important for motivation than motivation is for success.

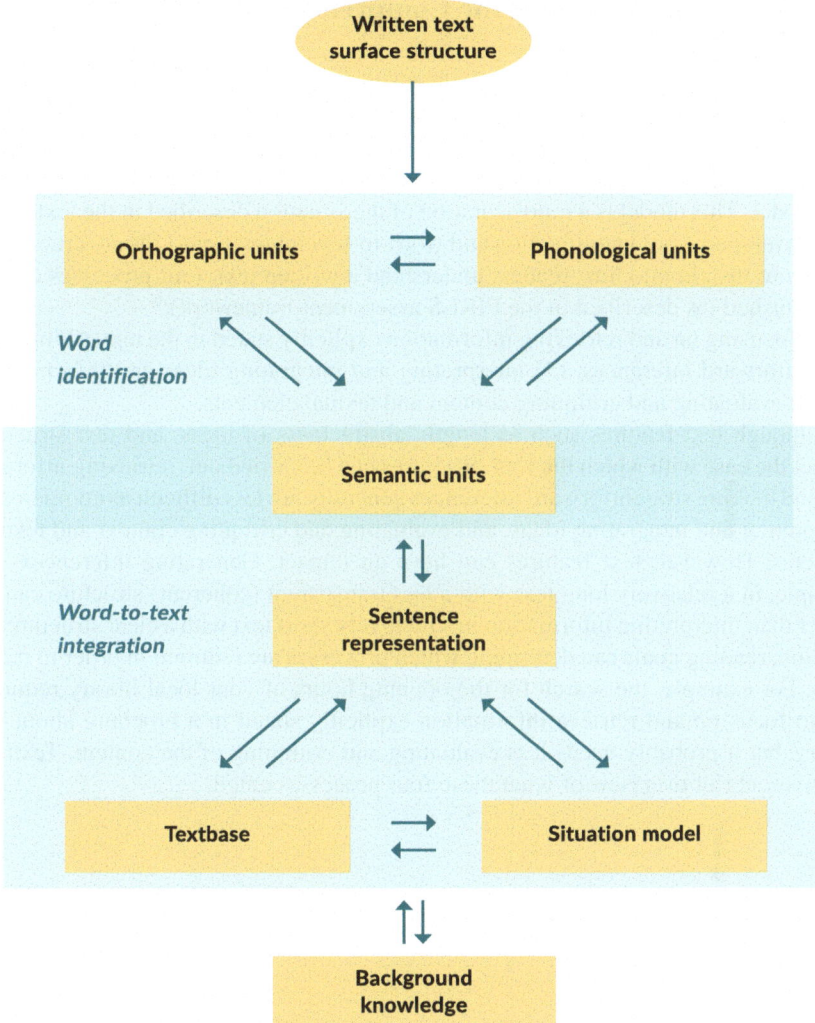

Fig. 1.1 A schematic overview of the comprehension process described in the Reading Systems Framework (RSF), with word identification and word-to-text integration as the two main subprocesses acting in parallel (*Note* This figure is an adapted version of the figure presented in Perfetti & Stafura[, 2014])

1.3   Four Main Processes for Comprehension

In the previous section, it has been shown that, at the surface level, readers use the text to create propositions and combine these propositions into a textbase. The textbase functions as a model of the information stated in the text. By incorporating relevant background knowledge, readers transform the textbase into a situation model. This model is a representation of the situation described in the text. Both well-developed word identification and word-to-text integration skills are crucial. To gain more insight into how readers understand a written text, four processes can be distinguished (as described in the PIRLS assessment framework):

(1) focusing on and retrieving information explicitly stated in the text, (2) making straightforward inferences, (3) interpreting and integrating ideas and information, and (4) evaluating and critiquing content and textual elements.

Although text features such as length, abstractness of ideas, and text structure impact the ease with which the four processes can be carried out, retrieving information and making straightforward inferences generally are less difficult as compared to interpreting and integrating ideas, and evaluating and critiquing context and textual elements. However, text features can have an impact. Generating inferences, for example, in a relatively long text with a less transparent (coherent) structure can be harder than interpreting information in a relatively short text with a clear structure. In addition, reading goals can determine which processes are required in order to reach them. For example, the search for the opening hours of your local library requires you to focus on and retrieve information explicitly stated in a brochure about the library, but it probably needs less evaluating and critiquing of the content. Textbox 1.4 gives a brief overview of what these four processes entail.

Textbox 1.4: The four main processes for text comprehension as described in the PIRLS assessment framework

1. Focus on and retrieve explicitly stated information
In focusing on and retrieving explicitly stated information, readers use various ways to locate and understand content that is relevant [to the reader's goal]. Typically, this type of text processing requires the reader to focus on the text at the word, phrase, and sentence levels in order to construct meaning. ... successful retrieval requires a fairly immediate or automatic understanding of the text.

2. Make straightforward inferences
Making inferences allows readers to move beyond the surface [features] of texts and to resolve the gaps in meaning that often occur. [Straightforward inferences require the reader to connect two or more propositions that are explicitly stated in the text. Although the necessary information is stated explicitly, the connection needed to understand the text has to be inferred.] Skilled readers often make these kinds of inferences... They may immediately connect two or more pieces of information, recognizing a relationship even though it is not stated in the text.

3. Interpret and integrate ideas and information
As readers interpret and integrate, they are attempting to construct a more specific or more complete understanding of the text by integrating personal knowledge and experience with meaning that resides within the text. ...as readers engage in this interpretive process, they are making connections that are not only implicit, but that may be open to some interpretation based on their own perspectives.

4. Evaluate and critique content and textual features
As readers evaluate the content and elements of a text, the focus shifts from constructing meaning to critically considering the text itself. Readers engaged in this process step back from a text in order to examine and critique it.

Textbox 1.5: Explanation of the term "didactic"

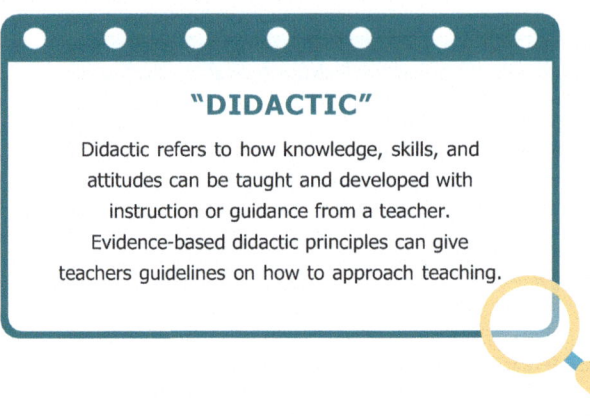

"DIDACTIC"

Didactic refers to how knowledge, skills, and
attitudes can be taught and developed with
instruction or guidance from a teacher.
Evidence-based didactic principles can give
teachers guidelines on how to approach teaching.

In addition to the two purposes of reading described briefly in Sect. 1.1 (reading for literary experience and reading to acquire and use information), these four comprehension processes are also distinguished within the PIRLS assessment framework. PIRLS results therefore provide teachers and policymakers with information on how well students are able to carry out these four processes in order to understand texts written to entertain readers (literary experience) or to teach them new information (acquire and use information). In Chapter 3, two PIRLS passages (one narrative for literary experience and one expository for acquiring and using information) will be addressed, providing examples of these four processes. Additionally, information will be shared on which skills children need to develop to successfully complete these processes and also offer didactic (see Textbox 1.5) suggestions, in order to help them develop better comprehension skills. In the next chapter, insights on evidence-based didactic principles are presented.

1.4 In summary

✓ Comprehending a written text requires the reader to identify the words used in the text, combine single word meanings into propositions, and subsequently create a coherent and adequate model of the text (i.e., textbase). Together with relevant background knowledge, this shallow textbase can be enhanced into a more in-depth situation model which depicts the situation described in the text.

✓ Within the PIRLS framework, two main purposes for reading can be distinguished: reading for literary experiences and reading to acquire and use information. In addition, four main comprehension processes can be distinguished for grade 4 students: focusing on and retrieving information explicitly stated in the text, making straightforward inferences, interpreting and integrating ideas and information, and evaluating and critiquing content and textual elements.

✓ Important factors that have proven to have an impact on how well a reader understands a text are: word identification abilities, language comprehension abilities, the use of reading comprehension strategies, and reading motivation.

Reading Tips

- **Title:** Understanding and teaching reading comprehension: A Handbook. **Authors and year:** Jane Oakhill, Kate Cain, & Carsten Elbro (2015). **Publisher:** Routledge.
- **Title:** Ending the reading wars: Reading acquisition from novice to expert. **Authors and year:** Anne Castles, Kathleen Rastle, & Kate Nation (2018). **Publisher:** Article in: Psychological Science in the Public Interest (Vol 19, Issue 1, pages 5–51)
- **Title:** Reading development and difficulties. **Authors and year:** Kate Cain (2010). **Publisher:** John Wiley And Sons Ltd.
- **Title:** Bringing words to life. Robust vocabulary instruction. **Authors and year:** Isabel Beck, Margaret McKeown, & Linda Kucan (2013). **Publisher:** Guilford Publications.
- **Title:** Developing reading comprehension. **Authors and year:** Paula Clarke, Emma Truelove, Charles Hulme, & Margaret Snowling (2014). **Publisher:** John Wiley & Sons, Ltd.
- **Title:** What is disciplinary literacy and why does it matter? **Authors and year:** Timothy Shanahan & Cynthia Shanahan (2012). **Publisher:** Article in: Topics in language disorders (Vol 32, Issue 1, pages 7–18)
- **Title:** Approaching difficulties in literacy development. **Authors and year:** Felicity Fletcher-Campbell, Janet Soler & Gavin Reid (Eds.) (2009). **Publisher:** The Open University

18 1 Theories of Reading Comprehension

References

Afflerbach, P., & Cho, B. (2009). Identifying and describing constructively responsive comprehension strategies in new and traditional forms of reading. In S. E. Israel & G. G. Duffy (Eds.), *Handbook of research on reading comprehension* (pp. 69–91). Routledge.

Andreassen, R., Jensen, M. S., & Bråten, I. (2017). Investigating self-regulated study strategies among postsecondary students with and without dyslexia: A diary method study. *Reading and Writing: An Interdisciplinary Journal, 30*(9), 1891–1916.

Chall, J. S., & Jacobs, V. A. (2003). The classic study on poor children's fourth-grade slump. *American educator, 27*(1), 14–15. https://www.aft.org/periodical/american-educator/spring-2003/classic-study-poor-childrens-fourth-grade-slump

Clinton, V., Taylor, T., Bajpayee, S., Davison, M. L., Carlson, S. E., & Seipel, B. (2020). Inferential comprehension differences between narrative and expository texts: A systematic review and meta-analysis. *Reading and Writing, 33*, 2223–2248.

Dyson, H., Best, W., Solity, J., & Hulme, C. (2017). Training mispronunciation correction and word meanings improves children's ability to learn to read words. *Scientific Studies of Reading, 21*(5), 392–407.

Gough, P. B., & Tunmer, W. E. (1986). Decoding, reading, and reading disability. *RASE: Remedial and Special Education, 7*(1), 6–10. https://doi.org/10.1177/074193258600700104

Hjetland, H. N., Lervåg, A., Lyster, S. A. H., Hagtvet, B. E., Hulme, C., & Melby-Lervåg, M. (2019). Pathways to reading comprehension: A longitudinal study from 4 to 9 years of age. *Journal of Educational Psychology, 111*(5), 751.

Kintsch, W. (1998). *Comprehension: A paradigm for cognition.* Cambridge University Press.

Kintsch, W., & Rawson, K. A. (2005). Comprehension. In M. J. Snowling & C. Hulme (Eds.), *The science of reading: A handbook* (pp. 211–226). Blackwell Pub.

McNamara, D. S., Ozuru, Y., & Floyd, R. G. (2011). Comprehension challenges in the fourth grade: The roles of text cohesion, text genre, and readers' prior knowledge. *International Electronic Journal of Elementary Education, 4*(1), 229–257.

Mol, S. E., & Bus, A. G. (2011). To read or not to read: A meta-analysis of print exposure from infancy to early adulthood. *Psychological Bulletin, 137*(2), 267.

Mullis, I. V., & Martin, M. O. (Eds.). (2019). *PIRLS 2021 assessment frameworks.* Boston College, TIMSS & PIRLS International Study Center. https://timssandpirls.bc.edu/pirls2021/frameworks/

Nagy, W. E., & Scott, J. A. (2000). Vocabulary processes. In M. L. Kamil, P. B. Mosenthal, P. D. Pearson, & R. Barr (Eds.), *Handbook of reading research* (Vol. 3, pp. 269–284). Lawrence Erlbaum Associates Publishers.

Patel, T. K., Snowling, M. J., & de Jong, P. F. (2004). A cross-linguistic comparison of children learning to read in English and Dutch. *Journal of Educational Psychology, 96*(4), 785–797.

Perfetti, C. (2007). Reading ability: Lexical quality to comprehension. *Scientific Studies of Reading, 11*(4), 357–383.

Perfetti, C., & Stafura, J. (2014). Word knowledge in a theory of reading comprehension. *Scientific Studies of Reading, 18*(1), 22–37.

Scarborough, H. S. (2001). Connecting early language and literacy to later reading (dis) abilities: Evidence, theory, and practice. In S. Neuman & D. Dickinson (Eds.), *Handbook for research in early literacy* (pp. 97–110). Guilford Press.

Toste, J. R., Didion, L., Peng, P., Filderman, M. J., & McClelland, A. M. (2020). A meta- analytic review of the relations between motivation and reading achievement for K–12 students. *Review of Educational Research, 90*(3), 420–456.

Van den Broek, P., Young, M., Tzeng, Y., & Linderholm, T. (1999). The landscape model of reading. In H. van Oostendorp & S. R. Goldman (Eds.), *The construction of mental representations during reading* (pp. 71–98). Erlbaum.

Verhoeven, L., van Leeuwe, J., & Vermeer, A. (2011). Vocabulary growth and reading development across the elementary school years. *Scientific Studies of Reading, 15*(1), 8–25.

Chapter 2
Evidence-Based Didactic Principles and Practical Teaching Suggestions

An Overview of Evidence-Based Didactic Principles for Reading Comprehension, Illustrated in Practical Lesson Suggestions

Abstract Based on scientific insights, five key didactic principles for teaching reading comprehension are discussed in this chapter: (1) Reading in a meaningful and functional context, (2) in-depth interaction about texts, (3) explicit instruction in reading strategies, (4) integrating reading tasks with other subjects, and (5) monitoring factors associated with reading comprehension and differentiating instruction. These didactic principles are outlined with examples and practical advice. Several of these didactic principles have already been incorporated in well-known didactic approaches. This chapter also describes some graphic organizers, that can be used as a tool to actively process the content of the text and therefore enhance comprehension.

Keywords Reading comprehension · Didactic principles · Practical guidelines · Didactic approaches · Graphic organizers

2.1 Introduction

Well-developed reading comprehension skills are a prerequisite in order to participate in the literate world we live in. Teaching children how to comprehend written language, therefore, is one of the most significant educational goals. It is, however, also one of the most challenging skills to teach children. Reading comprehension is not only an enormously complex process in which various underlying skills play a role (see Chapter 1), it is also a process that mainly takes place in the mind of the reader without being directly visible. Learning how to comprehend a written text is a skill that children do not acquire on their own, it is a process that requires professional guidance and support, first and foremost provided by their teachers.

Over the past decades, many studies have examined the ways in which children can best be taught how to understand written texts (Hebert et al., 2016; Okkinga et al., 2018). The results of these studies have led to the description of numerous evidence-based insights which have a positive effect on students' reading comprehension skills and their development. However, implementation of these insights by educational professionals such as teachers is not that simple. It is necessary to combine the conclusions of several studies on the same topic and subsequently derive the practical recommendations. The present chapter aims to help teachers apply scientific

© The Author(s) 2022
M. Bruggink et al., *Putting PIRLS to Use in Classrooms Across the Globe*, IEA Research for Educators 1, https://doi.org/10.1007/978-3-030-95266-2_2

insights into their daily reading activities by providing evidence-based didactic principles, and translate them into teaching approaches, examples, and didactic tools. In Sect. 2.2 we discuss five effective didactic principles, followed by well-known teaching approaches and, in Sect. 2.3, we provide an example of a reading lesson which combines (most of) these principles. In Sect. 2.4, we describe the use of organizers, tools that can be helpful in actively processing the content of the text, applying different didactic principles.

2.2 Evidence-Based Didactic Principles

As noted before, various research has been undertaken to identify effective principles in teaching reading comprehension. In our research, we started with a report in which various studies and meta-analyses on effective principles from the Flemish educational board were described (Merchie et al., 2019). From there, we extended our research by examining other studies known in the field. Based on this research, we have identified and outlined below, five key principles:

(1) Reading in a meaningful and functional context, (2) In-depth interaction about texts, (3) Explicit instruction in a limited set of reading strategies, (4) Integrating reading education with other subjects, and (5) Monitoring factors associated with reading comprehension and differentiating instruction.

2.2.1 Reading in a Meaningful and Functional Context

Reading is first and foremost a meaningful and functional activity (Pearson et al., 2020; Swanson et al., 2014; Wigfield et al., 2016). Whether it is because the reader reads for pleasure or personal interest in order to learn, or because it is required for participation in our society, readers always start reading with a goal. Teaching reading and specifically reading comprehension, therefore, should not take place in an isolated context, but rather in a meaningful and functional context. By doing so, students experience that reading and having well-developed comprehension skills can be important, valuable, and useful to them (Swanson et al., 2014). School-related reading activities must resemble real-life reading tasks. This can be achieved by taking three factors into account while teaching reading comprehension skills: reading materials, reading purposes, and reading approach. These must be authentic and resemble the way people normally read by being meaningful and functional (Berardo, 2006).

2.2.1.1   Authentic Reading Materials

In selecting reading materials, it is important to keep in mind that in order to be meaningful and functional they must be student-centered, interactive, intriguing, and based on daily life. This can be accomplished by selecting authentic reading materials that match students' interests or are related to the things they have learned before. But what are authentic reading materials? Bacon and Finnemann (1990) defined authentic materials as materials produced without any educational purpose and written by native speakers of the language of instruction. Lee (1995) suggested that these materials are considered more interesting by students because they were developed without an educational purpose and provide students with a more natural use of the language. In the case of reading comprehension, texts used for educational purposes often are written with a specific comprehension-related learning outcome in mind (e.g., practicing a specific strategy such as summarizing) and by doing so specific, natural traits of a language may vanish, or unnatural traits may be introduced. As a consequence, texts are perceived unnatural, without a true narrative, and not resembling texts that students encounter in their daily life.

Authentic reading materials can be found in all kinds of sources, such as non-fiction books, (graphic) novels, materials used in other school subjects such as biology, history, mathematics, and life sciences, instructions (e.g., manuals and recipes), biographies, letters or emails, newspaper articles, poems, and social media posts. To create a meaningful and functional context for students, it is important that students encounter various types of reading materials and learn how to read and comprehend them. Most teachers know about the importance of reading *a lot*, but *variation* in types of texts is also significantly related to students' reading performance (Donahue et al., 2001). By reading different types of texts on the same subject, not only is a clear meaningful and functional context provided, but children also broaden their knowledge of the subject and learn to deal with different types of texts (see Sect. 2.2.4).

Textbox 2.1: An example of using various authentic reading materials

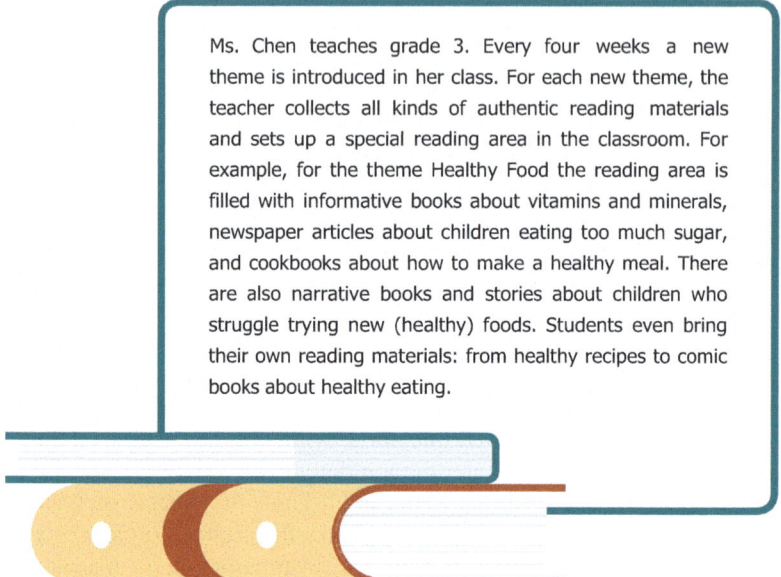

Ms. Chen teaches grade 3. Every four weeks a new theme is introduced in her class. For each new theme, the teacher collects all kinds of authentic reading materials and sets up a special reading area in the classroom. For example, for the theme Healthy Food the reading area is filled with informative books about vitamins and minerals, newspaper articles about children eating too much sugar, and cookbooks about how to make a healthy meal. There are also narrative books and stories about children who struggle trying new (healthy) foods. Students even bring their own reading materials: from healthy recipes to comic books about healthy eating.

2.2.1.2 Authentic reading purposes

As with reading materials, reading purposes (or, in other words, the reason why students are required to read a text) should be authentic. This can be achieved by designing tasks that are also student-centered, interactive, intriguing, and based on daily life. Tasks should be centered around clear purposes such as solving a problem, starting a discussion, or finding out what happens to the main character of the story. Setting clear reading purposes that are meaningful and functional enhances students' reading motivation and helps students to see why well- developed comprehension skills are important, valuable, and useful. However, in practice, reading purposes often do not resemble those set by students in real life such as acquiring information, but are centered around teaching a specific comprehension skill such as creating a model of the text or practicing a specific reading comprehension strategy (i.e., asking questions or summarizing, see Sect. 2.2.3). Take, for example, a biology text on the circulatory system (see Textbox 2.4). An authentic reading purpose or authentic reading goal would be to learn how blood travels through the body and to learn what the functions of the heart and lungs are. More specifically, an authentic reading purpose could be stated as: after reading the text, I know how blood travels through the body and what the function of the heart and lungs is. However, in practice, the purpose of reading such a text is often stated as: I can create a visual representation of the text. Although creating visual representations can be helpful in acquiring knowledge, in daily life, creating a visual representation is (almost) never the purpose of reading a text.

2.2.1.3 Authentic Reading Approach

The way in which a student reads a text should match the reason why they read it (reading purpose) and the type of text they read (reading material). In other words, the way that students read a text needs to be authentic. In Chapter 1, four main processes of reading comprehension were briefly described, namely: focusing on and retrieving information explicitly stated in the text, making straightforward inferences, interpreting and integrating ideas and information, and evaluating and critiquing content and textual elements. The approach used by the reader depends on his or her purpose, and the processes engaged depend on this purpose and the type of text. For example, when reading a recipe for making bread, it is important to explicitly retrieve information on how much flour, yeast, salt, and water you need and at what temperature you need to set the oven. Evaluating and critiquing the content or textual features of the recipe are less likely to be important. In instruction, it is important to match the reading approach to the approach most likely used in daily life. If the aim of the lesson is to practice a certain reading approach, this will have consequences for the choice of text.

2.2.2 In-Depth Interaction About Texts

Interacting on the content of the text (the meaning, the purpose, or the underlying relationships of the text) has a positive influence on students' reading comprehension (Pearson et al., 2020; Shanahan et al., 2010). This concerns not only interaction among students and their teacher, but also interaction between students themselves. In-depth interactions can take place before, during, and after reading a text and can take place in pairs, small groups, or with the whole class. By discussing the content of the text, and specifically the information needed to reach the reading goal, students gain new insights that they themselves did not think about, leading to a better understanding of the text. Discussions can be about the underlying arguments and views of a text, about acquiring and remembering information by discussing ideas, facts, clues, and conclusions from the text, or about the students' spontaneous and affective reactions while reading the text.

Interactions between the teacher and students that promote reading comprehension and reasoning about the text should be structured and content-oriented, and not be dominated by the teacher (Soter et al., 2008). This means the teacher's role is to guide students, encourage interaction, and also make sure the discussion is about the text and does not remain superficial. Teachers can use various ways to promote interactions with students or among students themselves. First, teachers can discuss a text by asking open-ended extended reasoning questions instead of presenting children with multiple choice literal comprehension questions. Extended reasoning questions ask readers to "analyze, evaluate, and pull together information from the passage(s) and involve finding causes/effects, making inferences, analyzing, and using logical reasoning" (Peterson's, 2008, p. 147). Examples of these extended reasoning questions are: why did the boy… ?, how do you think… ? and, what if the main character… ? Secondly, interactions can also be triggered by making comments which provoke a reaction, "I have never read anything so strange!". Both these extended reasoning questions and textbased comments can be used to scaffold children in moving from a textbased understanding to a more situational understanding of the text.

Creating sufficient opportunities for interaction is not an easy job. In order for interactions to be successful in enhancing comprehension skills, it is important that all students have sufficient opportunity to interact. Allowing sufficient thinking time for all students to come up with an answer is crucial. Not all students are instantly able to respond to open-ended questions or feel comfortable doing so. A second way in which it is more likely that all students can contribute is by creating small groups of students and using cooperative reading activities where each group member must contribute to achieve the group goal (Johnson & Johnson, 2009; Slavin, 2010). In a small group of three or four, students have more opportunities to speak and are more likely to interact with each other. An example of a cooperative reading activity can be seen in Textbox 2.2.

Textbox 2.2: A cooperative reading activity with role cards

Each group of students reads a text, and together they work on a reading task. Each group member has a specific role to clarify his or her responsibility in the group, for example:

- **Questioner** — asks questions about a part of the text a teammate has read
- **Illustrator** — draws images to represent the team's thinking about the text
- **Word builder** — ensures that all difficult words are understood and writes them down
- **Summarizer** — writes notes and summarizes the team's thinking about the text to the class

The teacher models each role and distributes role cards to each group, prior to the cooperative reading activity. Cards can be supplemented with conversation starters, tips, or graphic organizers. Teachers support students in their roles during the reading assignment.

(Source: Kagan & Kagan, 2009)

2.2.3   *Explicit Instruction in Reading Strategies*

As mentioned in Chapter 1, a reading strategy can be seen as a "mental tool" readers can use to support, monitor, and restore their understanding of the text (Afflerbach & Cho, 2009). Readers with strong comprehension skills are identified as readers who (unconsciously) use combinations of various reading comprehension strategies while reading.

Although reading strategy interventions can have large positive effects on reading comprehension (for meta-analyses see Rosenshine & Meister, 1994; Sencibaugh, 2007; Swanson, 1999), these effects are mostly found in controlled settings with small groups of students and highly trained researchers as instructors. Effects of strategy interventions in classroom settings with regular teachers as instructors are smaller (for a meta-analysis see Okkinga et al., 2018). In addition, it is important that teaching reading strategies should never be seen as a goal in itself, but as a means to achieve better comprehension. Strategies should be used while reading the text and building a textbase and situation model, or after reading the text to improve the quality of the textbase and/or situation model. An adequate situation model, serving the reading purpose, should be the goal.

Despite these limitations, using reading comprehension strategies can be an effective way to enhance comprehension, especially when these comprehension strategies are taught in a meaningful way. As previously noted, reading comprehension mostly takes place in the mind of the reader without being explicitly visible. This poses challenges in teaching how to read a text in order to comprehend it, and in teaching how to effectively use reading comprehension strategies. One effective way to do so is modeling. Modeling refers to "the process of offering behavior for imitation" (Tharp & Gallimore, 1988, p. 47). A common way to do so is by using thinking aloud procedures. Thinking aloud involves the process of making thoughts audible by saying what one is thinking while performing an action. In modeling reading comprehension strategies, an expert reader (mostly the teacher, but can also be done by a student) reads aloud part of the text and before, during and after reading indicates what they are thinking. By doing so, the expert not only shows students how to apply a strategy themselves, but also when to apply which strategies. Examples of how to model different strategies are presented in Textbox 2.3.

Although the National Reading Panel (2000) has distinguished more than 15 comprehension strategies, there is evidence for only a limited set of these strategies to have a positive effect on reading comprehension, especially when taught and used in combination (Okkinga et al., 2018; Pressley, 2006; Shanahan et al., 2010). Seven effective strategies are briefly described below.

1. Orienting on the text: making predictions and setting reading goals

    When orienting on a text, the reader views the text globally by looking at the text characteristics, like pictures, headings, layout, and paragraphs. By linking the information that they superficially extract from the text to their prior knowledge, the reader can make predictions about the type of text and its context. This allows them to set a reading goal and be prepared for reading the text. It is important that students do not make haphazard predictions and therefore possibly get a wrong idea of the text. In those circumstances, they would have to adjust their goals and expectations while reading. At elementary school level, predicting is best done with the guidance of the teacher.

2. Asking questions

    Asking students questions about a text is a good way to promote students' reading comprehension. Thinking about text-oriented questions, for example, questions about the sequence in the text, comparisons, opposites, similarities and differences, and causes and effects, contributes to reading comprehension. Even more effective is when students learn how to ask themselves these questions. When students ask their own questions out of curiosity, they are actively clarifying the text for themselves, becoming more aware of their own reading process, and staying motivated to read. Based on the prior knowledge and the predictions students make, questions will come up while reading: "What does this paragraph say?" "I don't understand. How has this happened?" "I wonder why... ?" etc.

3.   Visualizing the content of the text

To get a better grip on the content of the text, it helps to visualize or represent the text. This also contributes to generating further thoughts about the text. While reading, images may come to mind automatically and can be visualized by drawing or sketching. Also, stories can be acted out by a group of students, so that they can empathize with the characters. Relationships that are described in a text, for example causes and consequences or means and goals, can also be visualized by making schemes or mind maps (Figure 1.1 in Chapter 1 is an example and section 2.4 provides more information on graphic organizers).

4.   Recognizing text structure

Recognizing text structure helps students to interpret and understand the text in an effective and efficient way. When relationships between parts of a text are clarified using connectives (e.g., "because" or "therefore") to clarify a reason-consequence structure, readers do not have to infer the meaning of relationships themselves. Interpreting the text will cost less cognitive energy, reading times will be shorter, and readers will develop a better text comprehension (Degand & Sanders, 2002; Sanders & Noordman, 2000). This requires instruction about global text structure, the structure of a paragraph or sentence, and the use of connectives, for example, the structural features of a narrative text (characters, setting, goal, problem, plot, solution, and theme) or recognizing the words that indicate a certain relation (e.g., a sequence, comparison, contrast, cause-effect, or an enumeration). Text structure can be mapped in graphic organizers (see section 2.4).

5.   Making connections

To understand a text, a reader often has to "read between the lines." In other words, infer new information that is not literally written in the text. To do so, the reader has to relate essential information that they have read before to the new information in the text and combine this with their prior knowledge. This is not easy to teach, since a reader does this mostly automatically. Thinking out loud by the teacher helps students to learn how to make these connections themselves (modeling).

Textbox 2.3: Examples of teaching reading strategies by modeling

STRATEGY	EXAMPLE OF THE STRATEGY BEING MODELED BY A TEACHER
Orienting on the text	*When I read the title "Evi and her dreamhorse," it must be a story about a little girl and her horse. Looking at these pictures, I think something happened that made her sad. I wonder why...*
Asking questions	*"The second reason is..." Wait! So, what is the first reason mentioned in the text for why sleeping is healthy for us?*
Visualizing	*So the spider thinks he is stronger than the elephant [draw or think about a spider who thinks he has big muscles next to an elephant].*
Recognizing text structure	*It says "first" and "second" and "third." That means that a list is given. It might be a series of steps or a list of people or things.*
Making connections	*Hey, I've read about this before. Where was that again in the previous paragraph? / I already know something about this! I know that...*
Summarizing	*Hmm, so what is the most important thing in this section? Let's repeat what it says in one sentence...*

Continued next page...

Textbox 2.3: Examples of teaching reading strategies by modeling *(Contd.)*

Monitoring and clarifying comprehension	*"In most periods of the Earth's history the climate was very different from ours." Climate, what does that mean? Let's read further, maybe that gives me a clue: "The Earth's climate is changing. The average temperature on earth has risen over the past 100 years. Also the rainfall has changed." Ah, it has something to do with the weather on Earth.*

6. Summarizing

By summarizing a text, in any way whatsoever, the reader must think about the essence of a text and discard irrelevant matters. By summarizing a text together in interaction, students can discuss what they think is most important. The feedback of a teacher or other students while summarizing may lead to a better understanding of the text. By summarizing, students remember the essence of a text better, which is useful when reading about a subject you have to study, for example, the Middle Ages. A summary can be a written piece of text or a diagram with drawings (see section 2.4). Summarizing can also be done by retelling a story or recalling an expository piece aloud.

7. Monitoring and clarifying comprehension

While reading, comprehension problems may arise, for example, when the reader does not know the meaning of a word or does not understand a sentence or part of the text. When the reader monitors their own comprehension of the text, certain recovery strategies can be used to clarify things. At word level, students can use word learning strategies. These are strategies to find out the meaning of the word yourself. Sometimes the meaning of a word can be deduced from its context. Therefore, it is useful to read the sentence or part of the text again. Another strategy is to segment the word into parts. Prefixes, suffixes, and base words can sometimes give clues about the meaning, for example, the word "unre-liability" (un-rely-able-ity). Also, students should understand it is not always necessary to know all the words to comprehend a text. When comprehension problems occur at the sentence level, it can be effective to reread the sentences around it. Again, teaching to monitor your own reading comprehension is best done by modeling.

2.2.4 *Integrating Reading Education with Other Subjects*

Background knowledge is a crucial part of reading comprehension (see Chapter 1), so knowledge building is essential. The more knowledge students have about the world around them, the more they can rely on that while reading texts with new information. One way to build knowledge is to read all kinds of informative texts in other school subjects, such as geography, history, or (life) science. By reading texts from other school subjects, students not only acquire new knowledge, they also learn new subject-specific words. In addition, students learn to apply the reading skills they have learned before in new informative texts. Also, the integration of reading with other subjects often ensures that students become more engaged and motivated readers. In Textbox 2.4 the integration of reading education with other subjects is illustrated by an example lesson.

Textbox 2.4: An example of integrating reading comprehension and health science

Mrs. Smith's grade 6 students are learning about the circulatory system in health science. To arouse the curiosity of the children, Mrs. Smith brought a blood pressure monitor and measures her own blood pressure: 130 over 74. This immediately raises questions among the students: What does that mean? What is blood pressure anyway? A conversation about the blood in your body starts. The students speak all about their experiences with bloody wounds and what they know about blood. The teacher also talks about her experiences and explicitly addresses and explains a number of possibly unknown words (such as blood vessels) that also appear in the text they are about to read. The prior knowledge has been activated.

The students are motivated to learn more about the blood circulatory system. Mrs. Smith introduces the informative text from the health sciences textbook. The teacher and the students look at the headings and the pictures together and predict what the text will be about. The reading purpose is clear to all students;

Continued next page…

Textbox 2.4: An example of integrating reading comprehension and health science *(Contd.)*

after reading the text, they know how blood travels through the body and what the functions of the heart and lungs are.

Students read the text aloud in pairs. One reads, the other asks a question about the part that is read. To help them with that, the teacher created cards with introductions, for example: What I'm wondering about this piece of text is? ... or how come? The two students answer the question, which creates interaction between the students on the content of the text. The questions they cannot answer are written down to discuss with the teacher and other classmates later on. Students are used to reading in pairs like this; it is the same as in the reading lessons.

Once all students have read the text, Mrs. Smith suggests they draw a picture of the circulatory system to make sure they remember the information. She draws a human body on a large sheet of paper, and together they read the text again. While reading and thinking aloud, the teacher writes down the correct information in the drawing. With arrows, she indicates the direction of the blood. She draws lungs and adds: "Oxygen is absorbed into the blood through the alveoli." During the lesson, she increasingly leaves it to the students as to which information should be added to a particular part of the drawing. The teacher checks whether everyone agrees. Is this information complete? How can we describe it better? What does the text say about that? When they are finished, the drawing will be hung up in the classroom. In the next health science lesson, the teacher first takes the drawing out to review this newly acquired knowledge.

Reading can also very naturally be integrated with writing. Instruction in reading comprehension can have a positive effect on the quality of students' writing. Instruction in writing also leads to better reading comprehension. Students draw on similar knowledge representations and cognitive processes when they read and write (Graham & Hebert, 2010; Graham et al., 2018). Activities that integrate the two language skills can be: writing about the continuation of the story by using your imagination, writing summaries, writing notes, and answering or generating questions about a text in writing.

2.2.5 *Monitoring Factors Associated with Reading Comprehension and Differentiating Instruction*

How well a student is understanding texts can be monitored in various ways. The most obvious way is to take a written reading comprehension test. These summative tests often consist of texts and questions, or texts followed by an assignment. The goal of a summative test is to assess what the student has achieved at the end of an educational program or period of study (such as school terms). Depending on the results, teachers can make decisions about the future reading lessons and the amount of attention needed for certain types of text or reading processes. Students may struggle with one or more factors of reading comprehension that they need to work on, such as decoding, vocabulary, and background knowledge, which will impact their results. In addition, students' use of strategies, motivation to read, and the degree to which they feel they have control over their own learning process should be considered, as these aspects also affect the reading results. To monitor this, a teacher can talk about students' reading process with them or observe how the students construct comprehension when they read and think out loud. Another way to gain insight into the reading process is to ask the student to explain their answers while answering questions about a text (Cain & Oakhill, 2006). With these more formative ways of testing, teachers gain more insight into the student's reading processes (Brookhart et al., 2010; Witmer et al., 2014). The purpose of formative assessment is not to determine the level of understanding, but to improve the future learning process by giving feedback. By using both types of tests (summative and formative), teachers can decide which students need extra attention and which aspects of reading need further work.

Monitoring students reveals student differences in their level of reading comprehension and in their educational needs. It is therefore necessary to differentiate between students. Differentiation can be sought in the choice of texts. A text should not be too difficult as students will become unmotivated and reading goals may not be achieved. On the other hand, students do not learn from texts that are too easy. The trick is to challenge the student at exactly the right level. Teachers can determine the difficulty of a text by looking at the proportion of unknown words, or its coherence and structure. As mentioned before, the use of connectives such as "although," "because," or "on the contrary" in a text has a positive effect on its readability. Students with little background knowledge, for example, benefit from highly coherent texts with a clear structure (Kamalski, 2007). Readers with a lot of prior knowledge do not need the text signals that make the relations explicit. Simplifying texts so that they match the level of the student is usually not a good idea; this often leads to poor, meaningless texts. Instead of adapting the texts for readers lacking comprehension skills, differentiation can also be achieved by giving explicit instruction in word meaning, the use of reading strategies, and text structure. This extra instruction can give students the extra help they need to understand the same texts as their classmates.

Textbox 2.5: An example of monitoring students' reading process

Planning conversations about reading books with individual students or a small group of students, can provide many insights for both the teacher and the students. Talks can be about what type of books the student enjoys to read and why, how they tackle certain difficulties in a text, or how they handle a book assignment. Reading-talks not only give teachers insight into the reading preferences and reading process of the student, teachers can also immediately provide the student with tips or reading materials and set reading goals.

2.3   Teaching Approaches Combining Didactic Principles

To ensure that reading comprehension is taught as effectively as possible, it is important to integrate the didactic principles as much as possible, for example, by reading an authentic text together, modeling how to enhance comprehension using one or two strategies, giving students a cooperative assignment about the text, and finally discussing their outcomes together. The principles reinforce each other. Some of the didactic principles have already been incorporated in a number of well-known teaching approaches. In the following sections, we describe three effective approaches in which (most of) these principles recur.

Didactic principles in practice

To illustrate how didactic principles can be implemented in practice, we have highlighted the principles in [...] throughout the example lesson below and in the suggestions in Chapter 3.

Textbox 2.6: An example of a reading lesson in which didactic principles for comprehension are integrated

In the past few weeks, Mr. Mehta and his grade 5 class have learned a lot about space and space traveling. The students learned about the solar system and how the planets move around the sun, calculated the distance between earth and different planets and stars, and watched an interview with André Kuipers, a Dutch astronaut who went to space twice. In addition, they came up with their own learning questions about gravity and floating in space. These questions were answered by using informative books, texts from the internet, and self-designed gravity experiments. Students even designed and tested their own space shuttle. Today a reading lesson is scheduled, and the students read an excerpt from an astronaut's diary [reading in a meaningful and functional context]. They read about his thoughts in the week before his departure for the space station and how he prepares for it.

Before reading the text:
Mr. Mehta orients on the text with his students: What kind of text is this? Have you ever read a diary before? Do you keep a diary yourself? What do you write in it? We are going to read a diary of an astronaut. What do we already know about astronauts? The teacher has students briefly activate their prior knowledge in groups of three. Taking turns, each group member tells something they know about astronauts [explicit strategy instruction: orienting on the text].

Continued next page...

Textbox 2.6: An example of a reading lesson in which didactic principles for comprehension are integrated *(Contd.)*

While reading the text:

The first two paragraphs (Monday and Tuesday in the diary) are read aloud by the teacher. This gives him the opportunity to think aloud [modeling] and demonstrate how an expert reads a text. In modeling, he focuses on how to ask yourself questions and how to relate information in the text to prior knowledge in order to enhance comprehension [explicit strategy instruction: asking questions and making connections].

He starts reading: "Today is Monday and the final adjustments to my spacesuit are being made. This afternoon at 2pm, I have to try on and test my suit for the last time. I actually cannot wait! It is all getting very real now."

Teacher: It is all getting very real now? What does he mean? Let me read it again. Trying on the suit for the last time... He's almost leaving for space... It is really going to happen now. I think he is very excited!

He reads further: "My 4-year-old daughter asks me why these spacesuits are so boring. Why don't they make it pink with butterflies on them? Good question, I don't really know the answer. Maybe I should introduce it to NASA (United States' space program). Did you know that such a suit is very heavy? It has to be solid, because it not only protects me from the pressure differences, but also from sunlight, radiation, and small meteorites."

Teacher: Ha, pressure differences! We've read about that before. There is no air pressure in space, but there is on Earth. So the suit protects him from that.

He continues: "This afternoon I also have my health check and fitness training. Then I will go out for dinner with my wife, Amy. We're going to our favorite restaurant, for the last time for now. I'm going to miss her so much."

Teacher: Hmm, I wonder if he can call her from space.

Continued next page...

Textbox 2.6: An example of a reading lesson in which didactic principles for comprehension are integrated *(Contd.)*

After briefly discussing the first two paragraphs, students read the next paragraphs aloud together in small groups, taking turns. One student reads, the other summarizes the part of the text, the next responds and completes the summary. One of the students also writes down the unfamiliar words to discuss with the class later on. In a few groups where the teacher knows there are students who have difficulty with reading comprehension, he observes the students and models summarizing [monitoring and differentiating].

After reading the text:
When each group has finished reading the text, the teacher starts a group discussion about the feelings of the writer.
Teacher: The day before he left for space, he got "restless" and "broke into a sweat." What does that mean? What other words in the text tell you how he is feeling? At the beginning of the week, he was so excited. What has changed? Imagine you were the astronaut. The moment of departure is slowly approaching. How do you feel? Can you imagine the astronaut's feelings? Have you ever had such feelings yourself when an exciting event came closer and closer? [in-depth interaction].

At the end of this reading lesson, the teacher hands out small notebooks and gives his students an assignment.
Teacher: Write in your own diary today. Don't just write down what you did or learned, but also how you felt or what it was like at the time. You can add anything to your diary throughout the day. You can also draw to explain situations. You decide whether your diary remains secret or whether you share it with your classmates. Perhaps there are students who want to keep a diary on a weekly or daily basis [integrating reading with other subjects].

2.3.1 Reciprocal Teaching

Reciprocal teaching is an approach where students gradually assume the role of teacher during reading sessions with a small group of students. In these sessions, students apply four reading strategies: predicting, asking questions, clarifying ambiguities, and summarizing. Before reciprocal teaching can be used successfully, teachers need to model the four strategies separately and students need time to practice them. Once students have learned the strategies, they take turns in leading a conversation about the meaning of a text. Several studies show a positive effect of reciprocal teaching on reading comprehension (Rosenshine & Meister, 1994; Spörer et al., 2009). It encourages students to be actively involved in the reading process and enables them to monitor their comprehension as they read.

2.3.2 Collaborative Strategic Reading (CSR)

A similar approach is Collaborative Strategic Reading (CSR): reciprocal teaching combined with collaborative learning. Researchers have found positive results for CSR on reading comprehension (Karabuga & Kaya, 2013; Klingner & Vaughn, 2000). With CSR, students learn to apply cognitive and metacognitive strategies, like previewing (orienting on) the text, monitoring and clarifying comprehension, and summarizing. Initially, teachers spend time teaching students to use these strategies. Once learned, students work together in small, heterogeneous groups where each group member is assigned a specific role, such as a reporter who summarizes the main ideas, or a leader who determines the best strategy to use. The teacher acts as a coach in CSR.

2.3.3 Concept-Oriented Reading Instruction (CORI)

Concept-Oriented Reading Instruction involves working on a scientific theme for a number of weeks. Students formulate learning questions around this theme and choose texts that can help them in answering these questions. After a few weeks they present the results of the learning questions to each other. Other learning areas such as history are integrated as much as possible. Again, the teacher acts as a coach and provides reading strategies and interesting books and texts at different levels to support students. Research shows positive effects of CORI on reading comprehension and reading motivation (Guthrie et al., 2007). By embedding reading comprehension in a science/physics theme, the reading tasks become functional, and transfer can take place. A disadvantage of CORI is that it often only concerns informative texts.

2.4   Using Organizers in Reading Lessons

After reading a text, meaningful reading assignments should take place in which students actively process the content of the text. Deeper processing of text content may identify weaknesses in the text models that students have created. The reader finds out which part or parts of the text are not understood completely and, by using reading strategies, tries to enhance comprehension of that specific part. Also, students remember the content of a text better when working on assignments that activate their understanding of the text. A tool to enable students to actively process the content of texts is the use of organizers, such as mind maps. With an organizer, the content of (parts of) the text is displayed in a graphical, structured way. Organizers clarify how pieces of information in the text are related to one another, or how new information is related to knowledge students already had. Using schematic representation of the text is a study technique that increases the effectiveness of learning (Robinson et al., 1995; Hall et al., 1992). With the use of organizers, the teacher can integrate several didactic principles into the reading lessons. For example, organizers can be helpful in using reading strategies such as visualizing and summarizing. Also, creating an organizer in pairs or small groups automatically initiates interaction and discussion between students about the content of a text. Moreover, teachers can monitor students' comprehension of a text while observing students discussing aloud and completing an organizer.

Depending on the type of text and reading goal, various organizers can be used to structure texts. In the following sections, we discuss a number of organizers: mind maps, tables, Venn diagrams, schemes, and story maps.

2.4.1   Mind Maps

Mind maps are often used to activate background knowledge before reading an informative text. Students think about what they know about the subject written in the center of the mind map. Thoughts are divided into categories and related to each other. After reading the text, this mind map can be supplemented with new information from the text. It is important to structure the information in the mind map, so that the relationships between words become clear (Fig. 2.1).

2.4.2   Tables

For informative texts that involve comparing different things from the same category, a table can be made. In such a table, similarities and differences are mapped in a structured way. For example, in a text with information about different animals, a table like in Fig. 2.2 can be filled out.

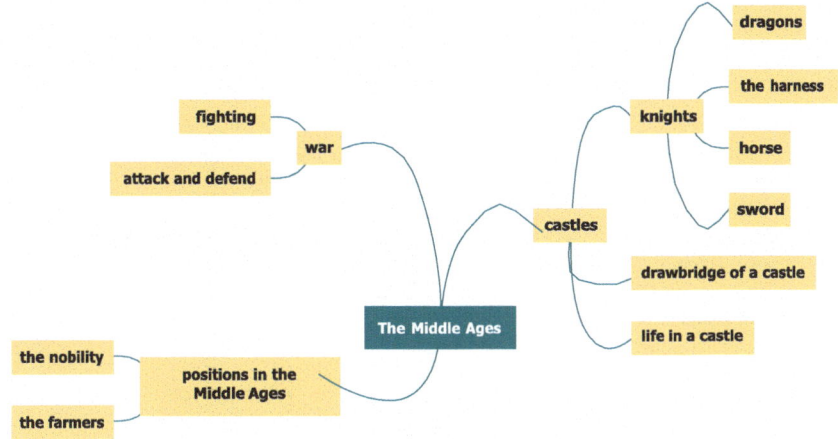

Fig. 2.1   An example of a mind map

	Is a pet	Can fly	Likes to swim	Has claws	Has hairs	Eats other animals
Lion				x	x	x
Cat	x			x	x	x
Goldfish	x		x			
Eagle		x		x		x

Fig. 2.2   An example of a table

2.4.3   *Venn Diagrams*

When only two concepts, phenomena, persons, animals, or things are compared in a text, a Venn diagram can be helpful to clarify the differences and similarities. The differences are written in the outer part of the circles, and the similarities in the overlapping part of the circles (Fig. 2.3).

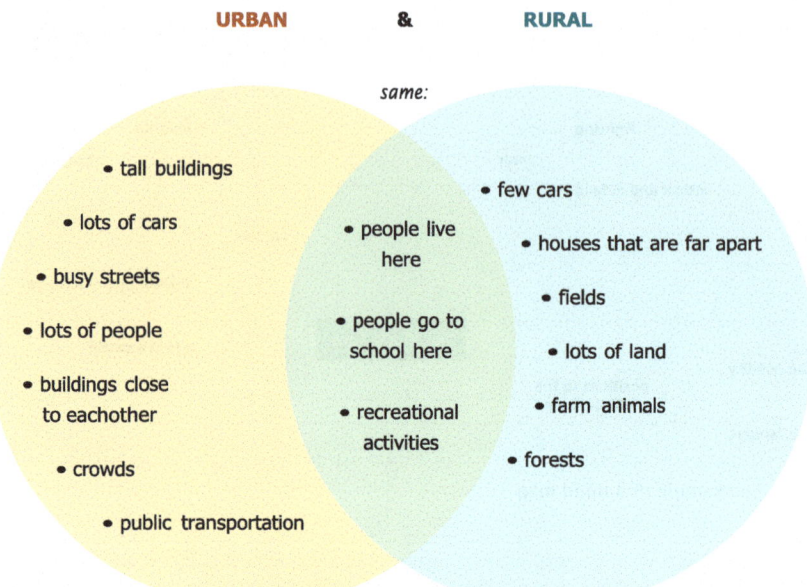

URBAN   &   RURAL

same:

- tall buildings
- lots of cars
- busy streets
- lots of people
- buildings close to eachother
- crowds
- public transportation

- people live here
- people go to school here
- recreational activities

- few cars
- houses that are far apart
- fields
- lots of land
- farm animals
- forests

Fig. 2.3 An example of a Venn diagram (*Note* This is an adapted version of the figure presented in https://nl.pinterest.com/pin/map-skills-location-social-studies-unit--431853051760868451/)

2.4.4   Schemes

Texts in which causes and consequences are discussed, can be represented in a scheme. Causes and consequences can be written in different boxes and connected by arrows. This type of organizer can also be used for texts where problems and solutions are described (Fig. 2.4).

2.4.5   Story Maps

A final example of an organizer is the story map. This is most suitable for narrative texts. By filling out a story map, students need to think about story elements like the characters, plot, setting, problem, and resolution of a story. There are basic story maps that focus on the beginning, middle, and end of the story. More advanced organizers also include elements like character traits or detailed information. With a story map, students can make a complete overview of a narrative text (Fig. 2.5).

2.5 In summary

✓ Five key, didactic principles for teaching reading comprehension are identified: Reading in a meaningful and functional context, in-depth interaction about texts, explicit instruction in reading strategies, integrating reading tasks with other subjects, and monitoring factors associated with reading comprehension and differentiating instruction.

✓ Reading comprehension instruction is most effective when (most of) these didactic principles are combined. Examples of effective didactic approaches are reciprocal teaching, Collaborative Strategic Reading (CSR), and Concept-Oriented Reading Instruction (CORI).

✓ Graphic organizers can be used as tools to actively processes the content of the text by structuring the most important information and therefore enhancing comprehension. Examples of graphic organizers are mind maps, tables, Venn diagrams, schemes, and story maps.

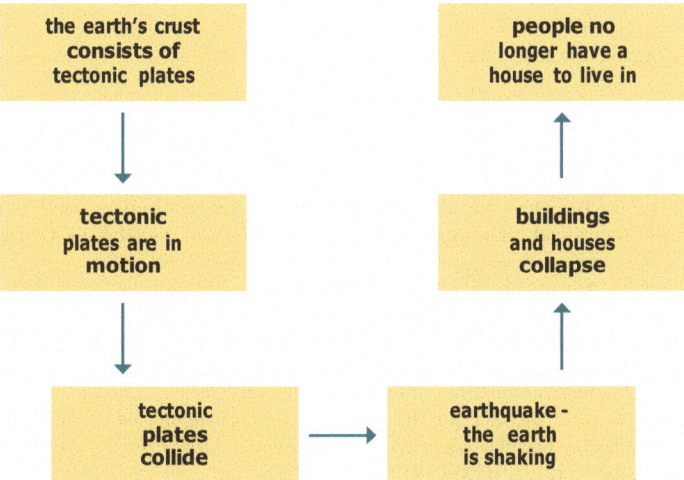

Fig. 2.4 An example of a scheme

SETTING	CHARACTERS	
In the woods and on the beach	Main character: Spider-Anansi	
	Other characters: The elephant and the whale	

BEGINNING	MIDDLE	END
Anansi challenges the elephant and whale to a tug of war	The tug of war starts, and the whale and elephant are pulling against each other and not against Anansi. The rope breaks and Anansi pretends to have won.	The elephant finds out that Anansi was not pulling the rope, but the whale. He gets very angry. Anansi flees and hides in people's houses.
Details	*Details*	*Details*
Anansi argues with the elephant and the whale	Anansi gives one end of the rope to the elephant in the forest and the other end to the whale in the sea.	A monkey has seen the tug of war from the treetops and tells the elephant what really happened.
The tug of war is tomorrow at 10am		

Fig. 2.5 An example of a story map

References

Afflerbach, P., & Cho, B. (2009). Identifying and describing constructively responsive comprehension strategies in new and traditional forms of reading. In S. E. Israel & G. G. Duffy (Eds.), *Handbook of research on reading comprehension* (pp. 69–91). Routledge.

Bacon, S. M., & Finneman, M. D. (1990). A study of the attitudes, motives and strategies of university foreign-language students and their disposition to authentic oral and written input. *Modern Language Journal, 74*, 459–473.

Berardo, S. A. (2006). The use of authentic materials in the teaching of reading. *The reading matrix, 6*(2). https://readingmatrix.com/articles/berardo/article.pdf

Brookhart, S. M., Moss, C. M., & Long, B. A. (2010). Teacher inquiry into formative assessment practices in remedial reading classrooms. *Assessment in Education: Principles, Policy & Practice, 17*, 41–58. https://doi.org/10.1080/09695940903565545

Cain, K., & Oakhill, J. (2006). Assessment matters: Issues in the measurement of reading comprehension. *British Journal of Educational Psychology, 76*(4), 697–708.

Degand, L., & Sanders, T. (2002). The impact of relational markers on expository text comprehension in L1 and L2. *Reading and Writing: An Interdisciplinary Journal, 15*(7), 739–757.

Donahue, P. L., Finnegan, R. J., Lutkus, A. D., Allen, N. L., & Campbell, J. R. (2001). *The nation's report card: Fourth-grade reading 2000* (NCES 2001–499). National Center for Education Statistics, U.S. Department of Education.

Graham, S., & Hebert, M. (2010). *Writing to read: Evidence for how writing can improve reading.* Carnegie Corporation of New York.

Graham, S., Liu, X., Bartlett, B., Ng, C., Harris, K. R., Aitken, A., Barkel, A., Kavanaugh, K., & Talukdar, J. (2018). Reading for writing: A meta-analysis of the impact of reading interventions on writing. *Review of Educational Research, 88*(2), 243–284.

Guthrie, J. T., McRae, A., & Klauda, S. L. (2007). Contributions of concept-oriented reading instruction to knowledge about interventions for motivations in reading. *Educational Psychologist, 42*(4), 237–250.

Hall, R. H., Dansereau, D. F., & Skaggs, L. P. (1992). Knowledge maps and the presentation of related information domains. *The Journal of Experimental Education, 61*, 5–18.

Hebert, M., Bohaty, J. J., Nelson, J. R., & Brown, J. (2016). The effects of text structure instruction on expository reading comprehension: A meta-analysis. *Journal of Educational Psychology, 108*(5), 609–629.

Johnson, D. W., & Johnson, R. T. (2009). An educational psychology success story: Social interdependence theory and cooperative learning. *Educational Researcher, 38*(5), 365–379.

Kamalski, J. (2007). *Coherence marking, comprehension and persuasion. On the processing and representation of discourse.* Dissertation. Utrecht University.

Karabuga, F., & Kaya, E. S. (2013). Collaborative strategic reading practice with adult EFL learners: A collaborative and reflective approach to reading. *Procedia-Social and Behavioral Sciences, 106*, 621–630.

Klingner, J. K., & Vaughn, S. (2000). The helping behaviors of fifth graders while using collaborative strategic reading during ESL content classes. *Tesol Quarterly, 34*(1), 69–98.

Lee, W. Y. (1995). Authenticity revisited: Text authenticity and learner authenticity. *ELT Journal, 49*(4), 323–328.

Merchie, E., Gobyn, S., De Bruyne, E., De Smedt, F., Schiepers, M., Vanbuel, M., Ghesquière, P., Van den Branden, K., & Van Keer, H. (2019). *Effectieve, eigentijdse begrijpend leesdidactiek in het basisonderwijs.* [Effective, contemporary reading comprehension didactics in primary education]. VLOR Vlaamse Onderwijsraad.

National Reading Panel. (2000). *Teaching children to read: An evidence-based assessment of the scientific research literature on reading and its implications for reading instruction: Reports of the subgroups.* National Institute of Child Health and Human Development, National Institutes of Health.

Okkinga, M., Van Steensel, R., Van Gelderen, A., Van Schooten, E., Sleegers, P. J. C., & Arends, L. R. (2018). Effectiveness of reading-strategy interventions in whole classrooms: A meta-analysis. *Educational Psychological Review, 30*(4), 1215–1239.

Pearson, P., Palincsar, A., Biancarosa, G., & Berman, A. (2020). *Reaping the rewards of the Reading for Understanding Initiative.* National Academy of Education.

Peterson's. (2008). *Master critical thinking for the SAT.* Peterson's Nelnet Co.

Pressley, M. (2006). *Reading instruction that works: The case for balanced teaching.* Guilford Press.

Robinson, D. H., & Kiewra, K. A. (1995). Visual argument: Graphic organizers are superior to outlines in improving learning from text. *Journal of Educational Psychology, 87*(3), 455–467. https://doi.org/10.1037/0022-0663.87.3.455

Rosenshine, B., & Meister, C. (1994). Reciprocal teaching: A review of the research. *Review of Educational Research, 64*(4), 479–530.

Sanders, T., & Noordman, L. (2000). The role of coherence relations and their linguistic markers in text processing. *Discourse Processes, 29*, 37–60.

Sencibaugh, J. M. (2007). Meta-analysis of reading comprehension interventions for students with learning disabilities: Strategies and implications. *Reading Improvement, 44*(10), 6–22.

Shanahan, T., Callison, K., Carriere, C., Duke, N. K., Pearson, P. D., Schatschneider, C., & Torgesen, J. (2010). *Improving reading comprehension in kindergarten through 3rd grade: A practice guide* (NCEE 2010–4038). National Center for Educational Evaluation and Regional Assistance, Institute of Education Sciences, U.S. Department of Education.

Slavin, R. E. (2010). Co-operative learning: What makes group-work work? In H. Dumont, D. Istance, & F. Benavides (Eds.), *The nature of learning: Using research to inspire practice* (pp. 161–177). OECD Publishing.

Soter, A. O., Wilkinson, I. A., Murphy, P. K., Rudge, L., Reninger, K., & Edwards, M. (2008). What the discourse tells us: Talk and indicators of high-level comprehension. *International Journal of Educational Research, 47*(6), 372–391.

Spörer, N., Brunstein, J. C., & Kieschke, U. L. F. (2009). Improving students' reading comprehension skills: Effects of strategy instruction and reciprocal teaching. *Learning and Instruction, 19*(3), 272–286.

Swanson, E., Hairrell, A., Kent, S., Ciullo, S., Wanzek, J. A., & Vaughn, S. (2014). A synthesis and meta-analysis of reading interventions using social studies content for students with learning disabilities. *Journal of Learning Disabilities, 47*, 178–195. https://doi.org/10.1177/002221941 2451131

Swanson, H. L. (1999). Reading research for students with LD: A meta-analysis of intervention outcomes. *Journal of Learning Disabilities, 32*(6), 504–532.

Tharp, R. G., & Gallimore, R. (1988). *Rousing minds to life: Teaching, learning, and schooling in social context*. Cambridge University Press.

Wigfield, A., Gladstone, J. R., & Turci, L. (2016). Beyond cognition: Reading motivation and reading comprehension. *Child Development Perspectives, 10*(3), 190–195. https://doi.org/10.1111/cdep. 12184

Witmer, S. E., Duke, N. K., Billman, A. K., & Betts, J. (2014). Using assessment to improve early elementary students' knowledge and skills for comprehending informational text. *Journal of Applied School Psychology, 30*(3), 223–253. https://doi.org/10.1080/15377903.2014.924454

Chapter 3
Exploring Reading Comprehension Skills using PIRLS

Schematic Description of Two PIRLS Texts and Items

Abstract Using one narrative and one informative PIRLS text and their corresponding items, this chapter helps teachers gain insight into the four reading processes. The specific reading skills, vocabulary, and background knowledge required to answer each question are explained. The chapter illustrates which difficulties students may encounter in a text and how teachers can help their students by using the didactic principles described in Chapter 2. The schematic description of each item includes the international PIRLS average. Schools can compare this with their own national average using the PIRLS almanacs and see if they recognize these national results in the reading level of their own students.

Keywords Progress in International Reading Literacy Study (PIRLS) · Reading skills · Reading processes · Practical guidelines · PIRLS texts

3.1 Introduction

In this chapter we discuss two PIRLS texts to illustrate the four reading processes: (1) focusing on and retrieving information explicitly stated in the text, (2) making straightforward inferences, (3) interpreting and integrating ideas and information, and (4) evaluating and critiquing content and textual elements, and the vocabulary and background knowledge that is required to understand these types of texts. This chapter is not intended to provide a method for testing comprehension, or to use test material as a teaching tool. Rather, its purpose is to give teachers a better insight into the reading processes described in Chapter 1, and to give teachers more concrete suggestions for implementing the didactic principles described in Chapter 2. Through these insights and ideas, teachers can better determine which aspect of reading comprehension students need extra support on and how they can provide this support.

© The Author(s) 2022
M. Bruggink et al., *Putting PIRLS to Use in Classrooms Across the Globe*, IEA Research for Educators 1, https://doi.org/10.1007/978-3-030-95266-2_3

3.2 How to Read this Chapter

In the schematic description of the PIRLS items below (see Section 3.3), we discuss each item from two publicly released PIRLS texts. Descriptions are provided for what students need to know or do in terms of reading skills, vocabulary, and background knowledge, to answer the question correctly. The international PIRLS average per item is also given (percentage of students who received full or partial credit). Comparing the international average percent of correct item scores with the corresponding national average scores by using the PIRLS almanacs can give teachers an idea of the reading processes the students in their country do well on, and which ones they struggle with. Teachers can discuss these findings in their school team: Does the school team recognize these national results in their own students, based on their own tests and observations during reading instruction? Are there types of items/questions that their students have difficulty with? Are there a lot of students in the school who struggle with understanding texts due to low vocabulary levels or a lack of background knowledge? Teachers can look up the items associated with these reading processes or factors (vocabulary/ background knowledge) and see which didactic suggestions might work best. These suggestions can give teachers inspiration on how to help their students improve their reading comprehension skills. More detailed information about the didactic principles, which the suggestions are based on, can be found in Chapter 2. Textbox 3.1 illustrates how teachers can use the information in this chapter to make decisions about teaching reading comprehension.

Textbox 3.1: An example of a school process for improving teaching reading comprehension

Ms. Gonzales teaches grade 4. After studying the items from the text "Flowers on the Roof" and comparing her country's national averages in the almanacs with the international averages, she noticed that students in her country score below the international average for most of the items associated with the reading process "Examine and Evaluate Content, Language, and Textual Elements." She talks about this with her colleagues, and they recognize their own students in these results. Students in their school often have difficulty evaluating the content of texts. Questions like "Why would the writer write it like this?" or "What can you learn from this text?" are more challenging for them, and they do not seem to be used to thinking about texts in this way. Ms. Gonzales reads the didactic suggestions that are given for the items about "evaluating" and collects some ideas to share with her colleagues. In the next teacher meeting, after reading about and discussing evidence-based didactic principles, the team decides to take more time for discussions to evaluate the text in their reading lessons [in-depth interaction]. They also intend to demonstrate, by modeling, how students can ask questions about the text to enhance text comprehension [explicit strategy instruction: asking questions]. By observing each other's reading lessons, teachers give each other feedback on how to model this reading strategy. For the students who struggle with texts due to their vocabulary, the teachers decide to select the unknown words in advance and explain them in various ways to small groups of students [monitoring and differentiating]. When they read the text with the whole class, these students have already been introduced to the unknown words in the text.

3.3 Schematic Description of Two PIRLS Texts and Items

3.3.1 "Flowers on the Roof"—By Ingibjörg Sigurdardóttir

"Flowers on the Roof" is a narrative text, and the reading purpose is to read for literary experience. The story is about an elderly woman (Granny Gun) who is more or less forced to move from her farm to the city. She gets homesick in the city and decides to get as much of her old farm into her flat as possible, including the hens and the grass with flowers on the roof. The story is told by a boy who lives opposite her, and he describes how Granny tries to feel more at home (Tables 3.1, 3.2, 3.3, 3.4, 3.5, 3.6, 3.7, 3.8, 3.9, 3.10, 3.11, 3.12 and 3.13).

Flowers on the Roof

by Ingibjörg Sigurdardóttir

Shall I tell you about a granny I know? She's a really strange old lady, and so full of life! Her real name is Gunnjona, but I call her Granny Gunn. Before she moved into our block of flats she lived in the country. Her farmhouse was just like a doll's house. It had tiny little windows and the roof was covered with grass. And there were flowers growing on the roof too!

Granny Gunn had lived all on her own in the farmhouse but she was never lonely because she had many animals to play with: a cow, seven hens, two sheep and a cat.

One day Granny Gunn became ill.

"You aren't seriously ill, but you should move into town," the doctor had said. "It's not very wise to live here all alone. Your cow can't call me if you break your leg out in the yard!"

"I can look after myself!" Granny Gunn answered. But then she thought that maybe it would be fun to live in town.

"All right!" she said suddenly. "I'll move to town."

Soon she had sold her farm and bought an apartment in our block of flats.

But what was she going to do about the animals? She couldn't take them to town with her, could she?

Luckily, the people on the next farm kindly said that they would look after them. It was still very difficult for Granny Gunn to say goodbye to her animal friends. She was *so* sad that in the end she decided to take her cat, Robert, with her.

Granny Gunn packed all her things into a van and was soon on her way to her new home. She was very excited and really looking forward to seeing the town.

I was very excited, too! I couldn't wait to see who was going to move into the apartment opposite ours. Perhaps it would be another little boy for me to play with. But it was Granny Gunn. Still, at least she had a cat.

Granny Gunn wasn't too happy when she looked around her new flat.

"This is just dreadful!" she said. "The walls are all smooth and white. And just look at those windows! They're far too big!" She became very quiet.

"I'm off back home!" she said, and turned to leave.

Then she suddenly gave a little scream. Robert the cat had jumped out of the window!

"Don't worry," I said quickly. "He's only jumped out onto the balcony. Look."

Granny Gunn rushed past me onto the balcony. But when she got there, she forgot all about Robert. The balcony was huge, and she could see the mountains far away and even a bit of the sea. Granny Gunn crouched down so that she couldn't see any of the rooftops—only the mountains and the sky. Granny Gunn decided to stay after all.

But the next day when I went around to help her unpack, she still looked very unhappy.

"Are you upset because all your animals are so far away?" I asked her.

"I do rather miss them," she sighed.

"Then why don't you go and fetch them?" I asked.

Granny Gunn winked at me and gave me a funny grin.

There was no one at home when I came to visit her the next day. Granny Gunn had taken the bus out into the country.

That night I woke up to hear a strange cackling

sound coming up the stairs. What could it be? Of course! The hens! They must have been too frightened to go in the lift!

The next morning, I helped Granny Gunn feed the hens.

"I feel as if I'm back home," she said. "The hens are cackling all around me, and if I squint, I can easily imagine that the mountains I see are those near my farm. All that's missing is the smell of earth and grass." Suddenly she opened her eyes wide and sat up. Granny Gunn had clearly thought of something new.

"Well now," she said. "Don't you think it would be rather nice to have some grass on the roof? I think we'll have to go to town tomorrow!"

And that's exactly what we did.

When we got home, Granny Gunn carried the pieces of turf up onto the roof. She laid them out carefully, and fixed them so that they wouldn't fall off.

Granny Gunn is much happier now. She's made a bit of countryside here in the town. She's now as fond of her rooftop garden as she had been of her old farm. And there are flowers growing on the roof once more.

Granny Gunn is not like anyone else I know. She can do anything! There's only one thing that bothers her now. How is she going to get the cow into the lift?!

Table 3.1   Flowers on the Roof—Question 1: Identity of the narrator

Question	Who is telling the story? a. a granny b. a child c. a doctor d. a farmer
Correct answer	b
Percentage of students who received full credit (international average)	78%
Process of comprehension	Interpret and integrate ideas and information
Skills	To answer this question correctly, students need to be able to infer the narrator's identity from the sentence "Her real name is Gunnjona, but I call her Granny Gunn." It is likely a child will call an old lady "granny." Or students can infer the narrator's identity from the sentence "Perhaps it would be another little boy for me to play with."
Vocabulary	Students need to know that a granny is the same as a grandmother or grandma.
Didactic suggestion	When students have difficulty identifying the narrator, it could help to put themselves in the role of narrator. The student reads the sentences the narrator says out loud. "So you call this lady Granny Gunn. What kind of person do you think you are? Why do you think that? Let's read further, to see if you're right" [explicit strategy instruction: visualizing]. Also, by modeling asking questions, students gain more insight into the different characters of the story. "Who is this 'I' person in this story? Why does the 'I' person hope that it is another boy to play with?" [explicit strategy instruction: asking questions]. If students don't know the meaning of a granny, talk about what other words the word is similar to [monitoring and differentiating].

Table 3.2 Flowers on the Roof—Question 2: Granny's farmhouse

Question	Which of these is most like Granny Gunn's farmhouse?
	a. b. c. d.
Correct answer	c
Percentage of students who received full credit (international average)	78%
Process of comprehension	Make straightforward inferences
Skills	To answer this question correctly, students need to read this part of the text very carefully: "It had tiny little windows and the roof was covered with grass. And there were flowers growing on the roof too!" Students are asked to translate this information into a drawing.
Didactic suggestion	Visualize the content of the text together, while talking about the text. "It says, the house had tiny little windows. Let's try to draw a house with tiny little windows. Does the writer mention anything about the color of the house? No. So we don't know the color. But we do know something about the roof! What does the roof look like?" It is also possible to visualize the text mentally [explicit strategy instruction: visualizing].

Table 3.3 Flowers on the Roof—Question 3: The reason Granny should move

Question	Why did the doctor think that Granny Gunn should move to town? a. because she was lonely without her friends b. so she could live with her relatives c. because she could not take care of her animals d. in case she needed someone to look after her
Correct answer	d
Percentage of students who received full credit (international average)	76%
Process of comprehension	Make straightforward inferences
Skills	To answer this question correctly, students need to interpret this part of the text: "It's not very wise to live here all alone. Your cow can't call me if you break your leg out in the yard." Students have to infer that the doctor thinks she should move to town because there are people there who can look after her, in case she needs help.
Background knowledge	Students need to know about the difference in the number of people living in a town and in the countryside.
Didactic suggestion	To help students understand this part of the text, it can be helpful to discuss the difference between a town (where Granny moved to) and the countryside (where she came from). By creating a Venn diagram, together with the teacher or in pairs, the differences and similarities between a town and the countryside can be displayed. Filling in a table with characteristics of the city and the countryside can be useful as well. Students' prior knowledge on this subject is activated when working on a graphic organizer together, and can be linked to Granny's reason for moving [in-depth interaction].

Table 3.4 Flowers on the Roof—Question 4: Who offered to look after the animals

Question	Who offered to look after Granny Gunn's animals when she moved to town? a. he people on the next farm b. the doctor c. Granny Gunn's family d. Robert
Correct answer	a
Percentage of students who received full credit (international average)	83%
Process of comprehension	Focus on and retrieve explicitly stated information and ideas
Skills	To answer this question correctly, students should find the following sentence: "Luckily, the people on the next farm kindly said that they would look after them." This states explicitly who offered to take care of the animals.

(continued)

Table 3.4 (continued)

Didactic suggestion	When students have trouble finding this sentence, try to remind students what to do if they cannot find certain information in the text. Perhaps they can read a part of the text again, or read ahead in the text [explicit strategy instruction: monitoring and clarifying comprehension].

Table 3.5 Flowers on the Roof—Question 5: Why was Granny unhappy

Question	Granny Gunn did not like the walls and windows in her new flat. Why else was she unhappy? a. she was ill b. she missed her cat c. she did not like the balcony d. she felt homesick
Correct answer	d
Percentage of students who received full credit (international average)	67%
Process of comprehension	Make straightforward inferences
Skills	To answer this question correctly, students need to be able to interpret the sentences: "'Are you upset because all your animals are so far away?' I asked her. 'I do rather miss them,' she sighed." This scene outlines that she was homesick.
Background knowledge	Students need to know what it feels like to be homesick.
Didactic suggestion	Let students share their own experiences of missing someone, for example when they were staying with someone or were on vacation somewhere. Talk about their feelings when they were away. Relate students' own experiences of being homesick to Granny's feelings in the text [in-depth interaction; explicit strategy instruction: making connections].

Table 3.6 Flowers on the Roof—Question 6: Why Granny screamed

Question	Why did Granny Gunn scream when the cat jumped out of the window?
Correct answer	The response provides an appropriate inference for why Granny screamed. It demonstrates understanding that Granny did not know there was a balcony outside of her window. It may simply state that she did not know this, or the response may focus on the fact that she was afraid her cat would be hurt or could die.
Percentage of students who received full credit (international average)	57%
Process of comprehension	Make straightforward inferences

(continued)

Table 3.6 (continued)

Skills	To answer this question correctly, students need to read the part from "Then she suddenly gave a little scream" to "He's only jumped out onto the balcony. Look" and conclude from this and the fact that Granny lived in a flat, that Granny thought her cat would fall down, and that she didn't know there was a balcony.
Vocabulary	Students need to know what a balcony is.
Didactic suggestion	It can be helpful to visualize this part of the text by drawing pictures of the scene, like a comic book [explicit strategy instruction: visualizing]. Talk about this scene and Granny's reaction while visualizing the story [in-depth interaction]. When students are unfamiliar with the word "balcony," show them pictures of all kinds of balconies and talk about what kind of buildings have balconies and what you can do on a balcony [monitoring and differentiating].

Table 3.7 Flowers on the Roof—Question 7: Why Granny crouched down

Question	When Granny Gunn was on the balcony, she crouched down so that she could not see any of the rooftops— only the mountains and the sky. Why did she do this?	
Correct answer	The response demonstrates complete comprehension by integrating ideas from across the text to interpret Granny's feelings about the mountains and sky. The response provides a connection between Granny's view from the balcony and her home in the country. It may state that Granny was reminded of her home in the country when she saw the mountains and the sky. Or, the response may suggest that Granny could actually see the countryside where she had lived. For partial credit, the response demonstrates partial comprehension of Granny's feelings about the mountains and the sky. The response accurately describes Granny's feelings about the view from her balcony, or provides an appropriate explanation for why she did this. However, the response does not make a connection to her feelings about her home in the country.	
Percentage of students who received full credit (international average)	36%	Percentage of students who received partial credit (international average) 51%
Process of comprehension	Interpret and integrate ideas and information	
Skills	To get full credit for this answer, students should sense Granny's feelings in this scene. They can infer that from phrases like "wasn't too happy," "just dreadful," and "she became very quiet." Also, they need to infer the changes in her feelings from the last sentence in the scene on the balcony ("Granny Gunn decided to stay after all"). Students can conclude from this that Granny was less homesick after seeing the mountains and sky, as this view reminded her of home.	

(continued)

Table 3.7 (continued)

Didactic suggestion	When students have difficulty interpreting and integrating a scene, try to act out this part of the story with a couple of students and ask questions about the feelings Granny has and how they changed. "She became very quiet. How did she feel at the time, do you think?" [explicit strategy instruction: visualizing]. Stimulating students to ask themselves questions about the text can help them to understand this part better. Demonstrate aloud what kind of questions they can ask and how to answer them: "Why did she decide to stay after all? I thought she was homesick. The view of the mountains made her feel better. I wonder why?" [explicit strategy instruction: asking questions]. Work together with a group of students who have more difficulty with this, and let students take over asking questions more and more. Keep modeling asking questions for the students who continue to find this difficult [monitoring and differentiating].

Table 3.8 Flowers on the Roof—Question 8: Granny winked and grinned

Question	Find the part of the story by this picture of Granny Gunn: Why did Granny Gunn wink and grin at the little boy?
Correct answer	The response provides an appropriate inference for why Granny winked. It demonstrates understanding that Granny realized at that point that she could bring more of her animals to the city. It may simply state that she had an idea or a plan, or that she realizes the little boy had a good idea. The response may also simply indicate that Granny agrees with the little boy's idea, or it may describe that the idea was to bring more of her animals to the city. The response may accurately describe the little boy's idea that prompted her wink and grin.
Percentage of students who received full credit (international average)	64%
Process of comprehension	Make straightforward inferences
Skills	To answer this question correctly, students need to link the question of the narrator ("Then why don't you go and fetch them?") to Granny's nonverbal response. This question gave Granny an idea. When students read further, they find out what her idea is.
Background knowledge	Students need to know about the meaning of these nonverbal expressions such as winking and giving a grin, like having a mutual secret or a special (secret) idea.

(continued)

Table 3.8 (continued)

Didactic suggestion	Discuss the meaning of giving someone a wink and make a connection to the text. "Did somebody ever wink at you? Why do people do that? Why did Granny do that?" [in-depth interaction]. Read the part of the text out loud and model how to make connections with prior knowledge about the meaning of winking [explicit strategy instruction: making connections]. Use winking throughout the day for children who have difficulty with the meaning of a wink. Briefly discuss the meaning with these students [monitoring and differentiating].

Table 3.9 Flowers on the Roof—Question 9: How Granny made her new flat feel like home

Question	Write two ways in which Granny Gunn made her new flat feel like home.	
Correct answer	The response demonstrates complete comprehension of Granny's actions to make her flat feel like home. It provides any two of the following actions taken by Granny: • Actions related to her animals • Actions related to her cat • Actions related to her roof For partial credit, the response demonstrates partial comprehension of Granny's actions to make her flat feel like home and provides only one of the actions taken by Granny listed.	
Percentage of students who received full credit (international average)	63%	Percentage of students who received partial credit (international average) 82%
Process of comprehension	Focus on and retrieve explicitly stated information and ideas	
Skills	To get full credit for this answer, students need to read the last part of the text, relate this to the part they have read before, and select the two ways in which Granny Gunn made her new flat feel like home. Students need to understand that Granny picked up the hens and covered the roof with grass, so her new home looks more like her old one. What her old farm looked like and the fact that she doesn't feel at home is described earlier in the text.	
Didactic suggestion	Demonstrate out loud how to summarize or retell the story. To stimulate students to retell the story themselves, ask questions like "What happened first? And after that?" and write down the events in the correct order. Emphasize the relationship between the problem in the text (homesick) and the different solutions, for example, by creating a scheme. The next step is to teach students to ask these sorts of questions themselves and that by answering their own questions, they summarize the story [explicit strategy instruction: summarizing]. Students can also work in pairs or small groups and take turns summarizing a paragraph. After one student has summarized a paragraph, the other group members complete the summary and discuss how to improve the summary [in-depth interaction].	

Table 3.10 Flowers on the Roof—Question 10: How Granny feels at the end of the story

Question	At the end of the story, how did Granny Gunn feel about her new home?
Correct answer	The response provides an appropriate inference of Granny's feelings at the end of the story. It demonstrates understanding that Granny had a positive feeling about her new home at the end of the story.
Percentage of students who received full credit (international average)	83%
Process of comprehension	Make straightforward inferences
Skills	To answer this question correctly, students need to find the sentence "Granny Gun is much happier now" in the last part of the text. This sentence literally reflects how granny feels at the end of the story. Students can also conclude from the end of the text that Granny felt at home now.
Didactic suggestion	It can be helpful to reread the last part of the text together. By modeling, the teacher can show which part of the text holds the answer [explicit strategy instruction: monitoring and clarifying comprehension]. Or students can briefly discuss Granny's feelings in pairs and formulate an answer. Collect the answers and start a group discussion about Granny's feelings. Talk about the difference in the meaning of feelings, such as "relieved," "feeling at home," and "happy" [in-depth interaction].

Table 3.11 Flowers on the Roof—Question 11: The purpose of last line of the story

Question	The last line in the story is: "How is she going to get the cow into the lift?!" Why does the story finish with this question? a. to add a joke to the story b. to explain the moral of the story c. to make the story believable d. to help the reader understand what happened
Correct answer	a
Percentage of students who received full credit (international average)	59%
Process of comprehension	Examine and evaluate content, language, and textual elements
Skills	To answer this question correctly students should be able to interpret this sentence as a joke.
Didactic suggestion	When students have trouble interpreting these kinds of jokes, it is a good idea to start a discussion about the meaning and purpose of this sentence. Maybe the teacher can collect several texts with these kinds of jokes and talk about why the author added such jokes. Students can also think of their own jokes at the end of a text [in-depth interaction].

Table 3.12 Flowers on the Roof—Question 12: What were the little boy's feelings

Question	What were the little boy's feelings about Granny Gunn when she first moved in, and at the end of the story? Use what you have read to describe each feeling and explain why his feelings changed.	
Correct answer	For full credit (3 points), the response may describe the little boy's feelings about or impressions of Granny Gunn. The response demonstrates extensive comprehension by integrating ideas from across the text to interpret the little boy's feelings about Granny Gunn when she first moved in and at the end of the story, as well as why his feelings about her changed.	
	The response describes the little boy's negative feelings when Granny Gunn first moved in and the positive feelings he had at the end of the story. In addition, the response explains why his feelings changed using appropriate and specific information from the story. Often, his feelings at the end will be implied through the explanation for why his earlier feelings changed. Or the response describes the child's plausible feelings of empathy for Granny Gunn when she first moved in and at the end of the story, rather than feelings about her, explains why his feelings changed. For partial credit (2 points), the response demonstrates satisfactory comprehension of the little boy's feelings about Granny Gunn and why they changed. The response describes the little boy's negative feelings when Granny Gunn first moved in and the positive feelings he had at the end of the story. However, it does not explain why his feelings changed or may include only a vague or general reason for the change. Or the response describes one of his feelings (his negative feelings about Granny Gunn when she first moved in or his positive feelings about her at the end of the story) and explains why his feelings changed. The response does not demonstrate understanding of the progression of negative to positive feelings. Often, these responses will describe and explain his feelings at the end only. For partial credit (1 point), the response demonstrates limited comprehension of the little boy's feelings. The response describes his negative feelings about Granny Gunn when she first moved in or his positive feelings about her at the end of the story. Or the response explains why his feelings changed but does not describe either feeling.	
Percentage of students who received full credit (international average)	27%	Percentage of students who received partial credit (international average) 45%
Process of comprehension	Interpret and integrate ideas and information	
Skills	To get the full credit for this answer, students need to be able to interpret the (changed) feelings of the narrator during the whole story. For example, the disappointment when Granny moved in, instead of a boy to play with, or feelings of proudness and happiness at the end because Granny can do anything.	

(continued)

Table 3.12 (continued)

Didactic suggestion	Model how the boy is feeling, while reading the text out loud. For example, when reading the part, "Granny Gunn is not like anyone else I know. She can do anything!" model the feelings of the boy: "So the boy thinks Granny can do anything! He must feel happy she lives near him now. Or maybe he is proud of her, because she can do anything. I would be proud!" [explicit strategy instruction: making connections]. Students can also do this in pairs. One reads a part of the text and the other shares how they think the boy is feeling. Students complement each other [in-depth interaction]. Help pairs who have trouble comprehending the boy's feelings by searching for words and sentences in the text that are related to his feelings. Model how to infer the boy's feelings from that part of the text [monitoring and differentiating].

Table 3.13 Flowers on the Roof—Question 13: The lesson learned from the story

Question	Which of the following might you learn from this story? a. old people will never be happy if they change where they live b. you can make a new place feel like home if you bring familiar things with you c. you can get used to living with animals, even though they are noisy d. children and old people do not make good friends
Correct answer	b
Percentage of students who received full credit (international average)	70%
Process of comprehension	Examine and evaluate content, language, and textual elements
Skills	To answer this question correctly, students need to evaluate the underlying message of the story. Therefore, they need to understand the complete story about Granny.
Didactic suggestion	Start a discussion about what students can learn from a text. First, students can discuss this in small groups, for example, based on cards with questions such as "What would the main character have learned from the story?" or "If you were the writer of this story, what would your message be to the reader?" and later share their conclusions with the whole group [in-depth interaction]. Relate other stories about moving away to the story of Granny Gunn. Does this character also make the new place feel like home? How does he or she do that? What is the same, and what is different from Granny's story? What can you learn from this new story? [reading in a meaningful and functional context].

3.3.2 "Giant Tooth Mystery"—By Kate McMullan

"Giant Tooth Mystery" is an informative text, and the reading purpose is to acquire and use information. In short, it is about the discovery that years ago animals lived on earth that are now extinct. It starts with the fossils found by Bernard Palissy hundreds of years ago. He was thrown into prison for his new ideas about extinct creatures. Later, Gideon Mantell searched for evidence for his theory about a giant tooth that his wife found. Gideon believed this mystery tooth belonged to a giant reptile that no longer lives on earth. Years later, complete skeletons were found which turned out to be from creatures we now call dinosaurs (Tables 3.14, 3.15, 3.16, 3.17, 3.18, 3.19, 3.20, 3.21, 3.22, 3.23, 3.24, 3.25, 3.26 and 3.27).

The **GIANT** Tooth Mystery

A fossil is the remains of any creature or plant that lived on the Earth many, many years ago. People have been finding fossils for thousands of years in rocks and cliffs and beside lakes. We now know that some of these fossils were from dinosaurs.

Long ago, people who found huge fossils did not know what they were. Some thought the big bones came from large animals that they had seen or read about, such as hippos or elephants. But some of the bones people found were too big to have come from even the biggest hippo or elephant. These enormous bones led some people to believe in giants.

Hundreds of years ago in France, a man named Bernard Palissy had another idea. He was a famous pottery maker. When he went to make his pots, he found many tiny fossils in the clay. He studied the fossils and wrote that they were the remains of living creatures. This was not a new idea. But Bernard Palissy also wrote that some of these creatures no longer lived on earth. They had completely disappeared. They were extinct.

Was Bernard Palissy rewarded for his discovery? No! He was put in prison for his ideas.

As time went by, some people became more open to new ideas about how the world might have been long ago.

Then, in the 1820s, a huge fossil tooth was found in England. It is thought that Mary Ann Mantell, the wife of fossil expert Gideon Mantell was out for a walk when she saw what looked like a huge stone tooth. Mary Ann Mantell knew the big tooth was a fossil, and took it home to her husband.

When Gideon Mantell first looked at the fossil tooth, he thought it had belonged to a plant eater because

Fossil tooth sketched life-sized

it was flat and had ridges. It was worn down from chewing food. It was almost as big as the tooth of an elephant. But it looked nothing like an elephant's tooth.

Gideon Mantell could tell that the pieces of rock attached to the tooth were very old. He knew that it was the kind of rock where reptile fossils were found. Could the tooth have belonged to a giant, plant-eating reptile that chewed its food? A type of reptile that no longer lived on earth?

Gideon Mantell was really puzzled by the big tooth. No reptile that he knew about chewed its food. Reptiles gulped their food, and so their teeth didn't become worn down. It was a mystery.

Gideon Mantell took the tooth to a museum in London and showed it to other scientists. No one agreed with Gideon Mantell that it might be the tooth of a gigantic reptile.

Gideon Mantell tried to find a reptile that had a tooth that looked like the giant tooth. For a long time, he found nothing. Then one day he met a scientist who was studying iguanas. An iguana is a large plant-eating reptile found in Central and South America. It can grow to be more than five feet long. The scientist showed Gideon Mantell an iguana tooth. At last! Here was the tooth of a living reptile that looked like the mystery tooth. Only the fossil tooth was much, much bigger.

Iguana

A life-sized drawing of an iguana's tooth from Gideon Mantell's notebook

Now Gideon Mantell believed the fossil tooth had belonged to an animal that looked like an iguana. Only it wasn't five feet long. Gideon Mantell believed it was a hundred feet long! He named his creature *Iguanodon*. That means "iguana tooth".

Gideon Mantell did not have a whole *Iguanodon* skeleton. But from the bones he had collected over the years, he tried to figure out what one might have looked like. He thought the bones showed that the creature had walked on all four legs. He thought a pointed bone was a horn. He drew an *Iguanodon* with a horn on its nose.

What Gideon Mantell thought an Iguanodon looked like

Years later, several complete *Iguanodon* skeletons were found. They were only about thirty feet long. The bones showed that it walked on its hind legs some of the time. And what Gideon Mantell thought was a horn on its nose was really a spike on its "thumb"! Based on these discoveries, scientists changed their ideas about what the *Iguanodon* looked like.

Gideon Mantell made some mistakes. But he had made an important discovery, too. Since his first idea that the fossil tooth belonged to a plant-eating reptile, he spent many years gathering facts and evidence to prove his ideas were right. By making careful guesses along the way, Gideon Mantell was one of the first people to show that long ago, giant reptiles lived on earth. And then they became extinct.

Hundreds of years before, Bernard Palissy had been thrown in prison for saying nearly the same thing. But Gideon Mantell became famous. His discovery made people curious to find out more about these huge reptiles.

In 1842, a scientist named Richard Owen decided that these extinct reptiles needed a name of their own. He called them *Dinosauria*. This means "fearfully great lizard". Today we call them dinosaurs.

What scientists today think the Iguanodon looked like

Table 3.14 Giant Tooth Mystery—Question 1: What is a fossil

Question	What is a fossil? a. the surface of rocks and cliffs b. the bones of a giant c. the remains of very old living things d. the teeth of elephants
Correct answer	c
Percentage of students who received full credit (international average)	75%
Process of comprehension	Focus on and retrieve explicitly stated information
Skills	To answer this question correctly, students need to read and understand the following sentence: "A fossil is the remains of any creature or plant that lived on the Earth many, many years ago."
Vocabulary	Students who already know the meaning of the word "fossil" may have a slight head start in answering this question, but the answer can be taken literally from the text. Knowledge about the word "fossil" is therefore not necessary. Also, students need to know the meaning of the word "remains" to get an idea of what a fossil is, but again, this knowledge is not necessary to answer the question correctly.
Didactic suggestion	When students have trouble finding the answer in the text, reread the introduction of the text and rephrase the sentence that states what a fossil is out loud [explicit strategy instruction: monitoring and clarifying comprehension]. To illustrate this, show pictures of different types of fossils and talk about the characteristics of a fossil [in-depth interaction]. Before reading the rest of the text, it is recommended to orient on the text and talk about the pictures, the title, and what is said in the introduction: What could this text be about? What kind of text is it? What is the best way to read this text? [explicit strategy instruction: orienting on the text].

Table 3.15 Giant Tooth Mystery—Question 2: Why people believed in giants

Question	According to the article, why did some people long ago believe in giants?
Correct answer	The response demonstrates understanding that people long ago believed in giants because they found huge bones/skeletons/fossils.
Percentage of students who received full credit (international average)	53%
Process of comprehension	Make straightforward inferences
Skills	To answer this question correctly, students need to interpret the following sentences: "But some of the bones people found were too big to have come from even the biggest hippo or elephant. These enormous bones led people to believe in giants."

(continued)

Table 3.15 (continued)

Didactic suggestion	Discuss the meaning of "too big to have come from...." "The bones were too big. They couldn't be from a hippo or an elephant, because their bones are smaller than that. Can you imagine people thought the bones belonged to giants?" [in-depth interaction].

Table 3.16 Giant Tooth Mystery—Question 3: Where Palissy found fossils

Question	Where did Bernard Palissy find fossils? a. on the cliffs b. in the clay c. by a river d. on a path
Correct answer	b
Percentage of students who received full credit (international average)	71%
Process of comprehension	Focus on and retrieve explicitly stated information
Skills	To answer this question correctly, students should read the following sentence: "When he went to make his pots, he found many tiny fossils in the clay."
Didactic suggestion	When students have trouble finding the information, suggest they reread the part about Bernard Palissy again. The information is explicitly mentioned in this part of the text [explicit strategy instruction: monitoring and clarifying comprehension].

Table 3.17 Giant Tooth Mystery—Question 4: What was Palissy's new idea

Question	What was Bernard Palissy's new idea?
Correct answer	The response demonstrates understanding that Palissy's new idea was that some fossils belonged to animals that no longer lived on earth, had completely disappeared, or were extinct.
Percentage of students who received full credit (international average)	25%
Process of comprehension	Interpret and integrate ideas and information
Skills	To answer this question correctly, students need to interpret the following sentences: "This was not a new idea. But Bernard Palissy also wrote that some of these creatures no longer lived on earth. ... They were extinct." Students need to understand that "But Bernard Palissy also wrote..." contrasts with the previous sentence, and that the idea that the fossils came from extinct animals was new.

(continued)

Table 3.17 (continued)

Didactic suggestion	Focus on the connectives: "but... also..." The word "but" indicates a contradiction (this *was* a new idea) and the word "also" refers to an addition (these fossils were not only the remains of living creatures, but they were also the remains of *extinct* creatures) [explicit strategy instruction: recognizing text structure]. If needed, discuss the meaning of the word "idea" in this text and that there could be more than one idea or explanation for a phenomenon [monitoring and differentiating].

Table 3.18 Giant Tooth Mystery—Question 5: Why Palissy was imprisoned

Question	Why was Bernard Palissy put into prison? a. people were not open to new ideas. b. he copied his ideas from Gideon Mantell. c. he left tiny fossils in his pottery. d. studying fossils was forbidden in France.
Correct answer	a
Percentage of students who received full credit (international average)	54%
Process of comprehension	Make straightforward inferences
Skills	To answer this question correctly, students need to interpret the part about Bernard Palissy and understand why his ideas were new and controversial for the time.
Background knowledge	Students should know how people reacted to controversial ideas hundreds of years ago.
Didactic suggestion	Start a conversation about Bernard Palissy's new ideas and how people reacted to his ideas at that time if students have trouble understanding this part. Also, talk about how people would react to controversial ideas nowadays: Do we still put people into prison for having new ideas? What has changed? [in-depth interaction]. To elaborate on this topic, the teacher can offer other texts about certain controversial ideas of people in the past and present and about the freedom of speech [reading in a meaningful and functional context].

Table 3.19 Giant Tooth Mystery—Question 6: Who found the fossil tooth

Question	Who found the fossil tooth in England? a. Bernard Palissy b. Mary Ann Mantell c. Richard Owen d. Gideon Mantell
Correct answer	b
Percentage of students who received full credit (international average)	68%

(continued)

Table 3.19 (continued)

Process of comprehension	Focus on and retrieve explicitly stated information
Skills	To answer this question correctly, students should read the following sentences: "Then, in the 1820s, a huge fossil tooth was found in England. It is thought that Mary Ann Mantell … was out for a walk when she saw what looked like a huge stone tooth."
Didactic suggestion	Reread this part of the text with students and model how the information can be retrieved. Talk about who they thought found the fossil and what she did with it. Why did she take the fossil home? [explicit strategy instruction: monitoring and clarifying comprehension].

Table 3.20 Giant Tooth Mystery—Question 7: What made the tooth puzzling

Question	What did Gideon Mantell know about reptiles that made the fossil tooth puzzling? a. reptiles had no teeth. b. reptiles were found under rocks. c. reptiles lived long ago. d. reptiles gulped their food.
Correct answer	d
Percentage of students who received full credit (international average)	57%
Process of comprehension	Make straightforward inferences
Skills	To answer this question correctly, students have to connect and interpret two parts of information: (1) He found a tooth that was worn down, and (2) all reptiles he knew gulped their food and therefore their teeth didn't become worn down.
Didactic suggestion	Make a schematic visualization of this part of the text, for example, by drawing a picture of Gideon Mantell with two thinking clouds that show the two parts of information that made the tooth puzzling [explicit strategy instruction: visualizing]. Also, model how to make a connection between the worn down tooth and the fact Gideon didn't know any reptile that could have worn down teeth [explicit strategy instruction: making connections].

Table 3.21 Giant Tooth Mystery—Question 8: Which animal did the tooth belong to

Question	Gideon Mantell thought the tooth might have belonged to different types of animals. Complete the table to show what made him think this.		
Correct answer	Type of animal		What made him think this
	A plant eater		The tooth was flat with ridges
	A giant creature		The response identifies the large size of the fossil tooth (as big as an elephant's tooth)
	A reptile		The response indicates that:
			1) The rock in which it was found was the kind of rock where reptile fossils were found/it was found where reptiles had lived.
			2) The fossil tooth was similar to/looked like an iguana/reptile tooth.
	Partial credit may be given to students who correctly filled in one of the parts of this item.		
Percentage of students who received full credit (international average)	12%	Percentage of students who received partial credit (international average)	38%
Process of comprehension	Interpret and integrate ideas and information		
Skills	To answer this question correctly, students need to interpret the part where Gideon was puzzled by the big tooth. They have to find the arguments in the text that argue that the tooth belonged to a giant creature or to a reptile.		
Didactic suggestion	Divide the students into pairs and set up a discussion about who the tooth belonged to. One of the students argues the tooth belongs to a giant creature; the other one argues the tooth belongs to a reptile. "What arguments do you have? Think about what you have read in the text." Make sure the students formulate complete arguments related to the text [in-depth interaction]. For students who have trouble finding the arguments, model how to recognize certain relationships within the text, for example, by selecting the connectives "but," "and so," and "only" [explicit strategy instruction: recognizing text structure]. Students can also make a more extensive table together of several characteristics of the different types of animals. For this they can look up additional information in other texts, for example, in a biology textbook [integrating reading education with other subjects].		

Table 3.22 Giant Tooth Mystery—Question 9: Why Gideon took the tooth to a museum

Question	Why did Gideon Mantell take the tooth to a museum? a. to ask if the fossil belonged to the museum b. to prove that he was a fossil expert c. to hear what scientists thought of his idea d. to compare the tooth with others in the museum
Correct answer	c
Percentage of students who received full credit (international average)	58%
Process of comprehension	Make straightforward inferences
Skills	To answer this question correctly, students need to interpret the following sentences: "Gideon Mantell took the tooth to a museum in London and showed it to other scientists. No one agreed with Gideon Mantell that it might be the tooth of a giant reptile." Students need to infer that the second sentence points to sharing ideas.
Didactic suggestion	Reread this part of the text and model out loud by asking questions about how you interpret it. "He showed the tooth to the other scientists, and no one agreed with Gideon. How can they disagree? Do they know about his ideas? Gideon must have told them about his ideas." [explicit strategy instruction: asking questions].

Table 3.23 Giant Tooth Mystery—Question 10: Why seeing the tooth was important

Question	A scientist showed Gideon Mantell an iguana tooth. Why was this important to Gideon Mantell?
Correct answer	The response demonstrates understanding that the iguana tooth provided evidence that supported Gideon Mantell's theory that the fossil tooth might have belonged to a giant reptile. Or, the response demonstrates a more general understanding that the iguana tooth looked like the fossil tooth.
Percentage of students who received full credit (international average)	34%
Process of comprehension	Interpret and integrate ideas and information
Skills	To correctly answer this question, students need to integrate the information in the previous part of the text (where Gideon thought the tooth belonged to a giant reptile and was looking for evidence for that theory) and the information in the part of the text where he saw an iguana tooth that looked like his mystery tooth.
Vocabulary	Students need to know what an iguana is. Besides the explanation in the text (a large plant-eating reptile), they can look at the picture to learn what an iguana is or search for other pictures of iguanas in books or on the internet.

(continued)

Table 3.23 (continued)

Didactic suggestion	Summarize together what students know about Gideon and the tooth so far, for example, by asking questions: What is Gideon's theory about the mystery tooth? Who does he think this tooth belongs to? Is he sure about that? So, he's looking for evidence? Finally, he found a tooth that looks like his mystery tooth! [explicit strategy instruction: asking questions and summarizing].

Table 3.24 Giant Tooth Mystery—Question 11: What Gideon used to figure out what the Iguandon looked like

Question	What did Gideon Mantell use when trying to figure out what the Iguanodon looked like? a. Bones he collected b. Ideas from other scientists c. Pictures in books d. Teeth from other reptiles
Correct answer	a
Percentage of students who received full credit (international average)	57%
Process of comprehension	Focus on and retrieve explicitly stated information
Skills	To answer this question correctly, students should read the sentence "But from the bones he had collected over the years, he tried to figure out what one might have looked like" and imagine how he used the bones to find out what the Iguanodon looked like.
Didactic suggestion	If students have difficulty imagining how to use bones to mimic the appearance of an animal, show pictures of skeletons and talk about how to find out what an animal looks like based on his skeleton [explicit strategy instruction: visualizing].

Table 3.25 Giant Tooth Mystery—Question 12: Purpose of two Iguanodon pictures

Question	Look at the two pictures of the Iguanodon. What do they help you to understand?
Correct answer	The response demonstrates understanding that the pictures in the text show the changes in scientific ideas, or that the pictures show different people's ideas about the Iguanodon. The response may also indicate that the pictures illustrate the mistakes that Gideon Mantell or other people might have made.

(continued)

Table 3.25 (continued)

	For partial credit, the response demonstrates an understanding that the Iguanodons looked different in the two pictures, or the response describes a difference between the two pictures without reference to changes in scientific ideas or what different people might have believed. The response may also provide an explicit reference to one of the pictures without reference to changes in scientific ideas of what different people might have believed.		
Percentage of students who received full credit (international average)	10%	Percentage of students who received partial credit (international average)	22%
Process of comprehension	Examine and evaluate content, language, and textual elements		
Skills	To answer this question correctly, students need to understand that the two pictures reflect the Iguanodon as Gideon thought it looked like, and as present-day scientists think it looked like and that there are differences between the two appearances of the Iguanodon.		
Didactic suggestion	Place these two pictures side by side and together read the text about the Iguanodon as Gideon thought it looked like and as scientists today think it looked like. While reading, relate the text to the pictures and discuss the differences between the two drawings [in-depth interaction]. Also, by summarizing the last two pages of the text together in pairs or small groups, students gain more insight into the function of the two pictures. Each group member contributes to the summary by adding important information or providing feedback. Help students summarize by asking questions about the text or model how to summarize [explicit strategy instruction: summarizing].		

Table 3.26 Giant Tooth Mystery—Question 13: What the Iguanodon looked like

Question	Later discoveries proved that Gideon Mantell was wrong about what the Iguanodon looked like. Fill in the blanks to complete the table.		
Correct answer	What Gideon Mantell thought the Iguanodon looked like	What scientists today think the Iguanodon looked like	
	The Iguanodon walked on four legs	The Iguanodon (sometimes) walked/ stood on two/hind legs	
	The Iguanodon had a horn (on its head/face/ nose) OR, the spike was on its head/face/nose	The Iguanodon had a spike on its thumb	
	The Iguanodon was 100 feet long	The Iguanodon was 30 feet (9 meters) long	
	Partial credit may be given to students who correctly filled in one or two of the parts of this item.		
Percentage of students who received full credit (international average)	32%	Percentage of students who received 2 points (international average)	46%
		Percentage of students who received 1 point (international average)	59%

(continued)

Table 3.26 (continued)

Process of comprehension	Interpret and integrate ideas and information
Skills	To answer this question correctly, students need to interpret the descriptions of what Gideon thought the Iguanodon looked like and what present-day scientists think the Iguanodon looked like and compare these descriptions. They must also document this information in the relevant spaces in the answer grid. The pictures in the text can help in imagining the appearance of the Iguanodon.
Didactic suggestion	Students can work in pairs and discuss the differences and similarities of the two Iguanodon. They can make a Venn diagram to structure the differences and similarities in an organizer. To help students create such a diagram, teachers can fill in one or two differences and similarities in advance [in-depth interaction]. Help students who struggle in finding the differences and similarities in the text by modeling how to interpret and compare the information in the text [monitoring and differentiating].

Table 3.27 Giant Tooth Mystery—Question 14: What discovery proved Gideon wrong

Question	What were found that showed Gideon was wrong about what the Iguanodon looked like? a. more fossil teeth b. scientific drawings c. living *Iguanodons* d. whole skeletons
Correct answer	d
Percentage of students who received full credit (international average)	52%
Process of comprehension	Make straightforward inferences
Skills	To answer this question correctly, students need to interpret the following part of the text: "Years later, several complete Iguanodon skeletons were found. … Based on these ideas, scientists changed their ideas about what the Iguanodon looked like."
Vocabulary	Students need to know the meaning of the word "skeletons." This can be clarified by showing different pictures of skeletons, for example of a human or of a well-known animal.
Didactic suggestion	Read this part of the text out loud and model asking questions in order to better comprehend this part: What was thirty feet long? Who walked on his hind legs? [explicit strategy instruction: asking question]. Suggest creating a timeline to record the various information in the text about Bernard Palissy's ideas, Gideon's theory, and scientific discoveries in time. This shows how the information we have about dinosaurs got better and more specific over time. New information from other texts could also be added. Per group of students, for example, information can be found about one extinct animal: In what era did this animal live? What did it look like? Did people's understanding about the animal change over time? [explicit strategy instruction: visualizing].

Part II
Teaching Reading Comprehension in a Multilingual Classroom

Chapter 4
Reading Comprehension and Multilingual Students

Scientific Insights About Teaching Reading Comprehension to Multilingual Students

Abstract This chapter describes scientific insights about teaching reading comprehension specifically to multilingual students. The role of vocabulary and the first language is discussed. This chapter also includes didactic principles regarding teaching reading comprehension to second language learners: monitoring students' reading development, stimulating reading in both languages, developing students' second language lexical quality, teaching specific reading strategies, and using first language proficiency.

Keywords Reading comprehension · Multilingual students · Didactic principles · Practical guidelines

4.1 Introduction

More than half of the world's population speaks more than one language. Whether it be through migration, multiple language groups living in the same area, or a different reason, many people, including children, live multilingual lives. Distinctions can be made regarding degree of language exposure, the age of acquisition, and the order of acquisition. In this chapter, we take a broad view of multilingualism: multilingual students are those able to express themselves and function in multiple languages. They are students who live or study in a multilingual environment for a variety of reasons. Students may speak the national language at school and a dialect or minority language at home or they may have a migrant family background and therefore speak a different language at home. The region where the students live may have multiple official languages, such as in Catalonia (Spain), South Africa, Canada, Curaçao, and Hong Kong, to name a few. In these cases, their education is often multilingual as well. There are also schools that choose to offer bilingual education, usually the national language in combination with a major international language such as English, Spanish, French, or Mandarin. In these cases, students become multilingual through going to school. In addition, there are many schools that only offer education in the national language, and students who speak another language at home thus learn to read in a language other than their mother tongue. Finally, there are countries with

© The Author(s) 2022

M. Bruggink et al., *Putting PIRLS to Use in Classrooms Across the Globe*, IEA Research for Educators 1, https://doi.org/10.1007/978-3-030-95266-2_4

a bilingual post-colonial setting, where the language in school is the post-colonial language that is not spoken at home or in the community (e.g., in Jamaica or Curaçao).

Textbox 4.1: Examples of multilingualism in different situations

George lives in Malaysia with his father and mother, the Kenyan ambassador. At home they speak Swahili and English. He goes to an English international school. His friends teach him some Malay when they go out.

Violeta and Roberto live in Chile. Most of the time they speak Spanish with their friends, family, and at school. But when they visit their grandparents, they speak Aymara.

Hatice's parents immigrated to The Netherlands from Turkey before she was born. At school she speaks Dutch, but at home she speaks mostly Turkish. Hatice listens to music and watches movies in English with her friends.

The nature of a child's linguistic environment influences how and when they learn their languages. Children who grow up with multiple languages in the home environment learn the different languages simultaneously. Another scenario is when children are sequentially bilingual: first learning the home language and then learning the school language when going to school. Children who migrate at a later age may already be quite advanced in their mother tongue (and even know how to read and write), before they start to learn their new country's language.

The different reasons for and timing of becoming multilingual result in varying degrees of fluency, both for home and school languages. For the classroom, this means that teachers are faced with and need to be aware of students' language proficiency in the home language as well as the school language, and the effect this has on students' reading comprehension skills. In essence, teaching reading comprehension to multilingual students is no different from teaching monolingual students. However, there are a number of specific aspects and challenges that teachers encounter in the multilingual classroom. In this chapter, we first describe theories regarding reading comprehension and multilingualism, and the impact of the first language (L1) on comprehension in the second language (L2). We then turn to classroom practice, showing how theory can be put to use in the curriculum.

4.2 Theory on Reading Comprehension and Multilingualism

In Chapter 1 of this book, we described theoretical perspectives on reading comprehension. These also apply to reading comprehension among multilingual students (Verhoeven & Van Leeuwe, 2012). In general, L2 readers (those who are reading in a language that is not their mother tongue), often have lower performance in reading comprehension in the second language (Melby-Lervåg & Lervåg, 2014), and this gap tends to be larger in the upper primary grades compared to the lower primary grades. The developmental paths, however, are quite similar (Schaars et al., 2019), and so are the contributions of abilities that predict individual variation in reading comprehension.

Learning to read in a language other than the L1 does not seem to cause many problems in general. Decoding skills have often been found to be similar in L1 and L2 learners (Mancilla-Martinez & Lesaux, 2010). The main reason for lower scores in reading comprehension and slower development of reading comprehension in L2 learners is the lower level of L2 vocabulary (Lervåg & Aukrust, 2010). Words in a student's vocabulary are not single units, but part of a network of words with many connections and cross-links between them. The more connections between words, the deeper the understanding of the target word. L2 learners often have a less-developed network in their L2 due to a narrower vocabulary breadth (number of words) and a weaker depth (quality of understanding) (Proctor et al., 2012). In addition, multilingual students' vocabulary knowledge is often distributed over their languages, although their vocabulary size is generally similar to (or more extensive than) monolingual students, their vocabulary breadth and depth in one language may lag behind their peers. For example, they may mostly know words for activities around the home in their L1, while mainly knowing words for activities at school in their L2. This can be challenging when reading stories about home situations in the school language.

Proficiency in the first language may have a positive transfer on L2 comprehension (Melby-Lervåg & Lervåg, 2011). This claim is based on the theory of linguistic interdependence (Cummins, 1979, 2001) that suggests that development in the L1 can help the development in the L2. For learning to read, for example, phonological awareness is an important precursor and highly related in L1 and L2. When students already know how to read in one language, this can help them in learning to read in another language (August & Shanahan, 2006); they are familiar with the concept of letters having meaning and forming words, and with the process of reading. Depending on the language, they may already know all or most of the letters (presuming both languages are written using the same script). For vocabulary, while a student may not know the label for a word in the L2, they can already be familiar with the concept and know the label in the L1, having already established at least partial lexical understanding of that word.

Johnny lives in South Africa. He speaks English at school and Afrikaans
at home. When his mother helps him with his math homework, he
uses the English math terms he has learned at school in their Afrikaans
conversation. When reading a story at school, Johnny struggles with
understanding the word "pajamas." A classmate explains that they are
the clothes you sleep in. "Oh, slaapklere!" Johnny replies. He just didn't
know the English word.

When the languages have more similarities, transfer will play a larger role, for
example from German to Dutch is easier than from German to Chinese. Students
may, for example, benefit from shared cognates: words in different languages that
sound similar and have similar meaning.

Environmental factors also play an important role in explaining L2 reading
comprehension. As in L1 comprehension, the home literacy environment is highly
important. Children should read, be read to, and see others reading, either in their
L1 or in their L2. Cultural differences may impact the reading motivation and attitudes of both parents and children regarding reading, which in turn can have an
impact on reading comprehension. When there are cultural differences between the
home and school environments, L2 learners may lack certain background knowledge that is needed for comprehension of school-based texts (Burgoyne et al., 2013;
Droop & Verhoeven, 2003). The quality of the linguistic input in the home environment is also an important factor in the L2 reading comprehension development
(Van den Bosch et al., 2020). For example, the conversations between parents and
children about various subjects play a role, as well as the number of books at home,
frequency of library visits, and playing rhyming games (Burgess, 2011). Exposure
to books from an early age is an important factor in becoming literate (Davidse et al.,
2011). Reading at home continues to be an important contributor to the development
of reading comprehension (Mol & Bus, 2011). Stimulating reading is important to
continue an upward spiral of causality (more reading, higher proficiency, higher
motivation, etc.).

As noted above, current theories suggest that many different facets play a role in L2 reading comprehension. However, it is important to not simply categorize children as L1 versus L2 readers, as the variation within L2 readers is very high.

Textbox 4.3: An example of students with varying shared understandings of cognates

> Limei moved from Beijing, China to Berlin, Germany with her parents a few months ago. She is now attending grade 2 at a local school. The German words are all very different than the Mandarin she speaks with her parents. Her classmate Jan is from The Netherlands, and he speaks Dutch at home. He recognizes many German words as being similar to Dutch, such as föhn – föhn [hairdryer] and man – Mann [man].

There are L2 readers with higher reading comprehension in their L2 than the reading comprehension of their L1 peers (Van den Bosch et al., 2019). In the end, the level of vocabulary is key to comprehension.

4.3 From Theory to Classroom Practices

Based on the scientific literature, we can formulate several classroom principles regarding reading comprehension in L2 learners. It is clear that the gateway to becoming a successful L2 reader is by gaining a large vocabulary, which is itself largely driven by reading. The reciprocal relationship between vocabulary and comprehension is clear and so, in classrooms, attention should be paid to both.

4.3.1   Monitoring the Abilities of the Children

The first principle is not a teaching principle, but one that relates to having insight into a child's capacities. A lower reading comprehension because of lower linguistic abilities in the L2 is not directly a reason for concern. It is a reason to pay attention to the development of the L2. It is crucial to monitor the development of reading comprehension over time. A lower score at one time point is far less of a concern when the child shows normal development over time. However, when development stagnates, this is a red flag. It is then relevant to find out whether the child also has problems in their L1, as this could point in the direction of a developmental language disorder (Genesee et al., 2004). Parents may be good informants of this latter aspect, starting from when a child enters the school—whether it be in grade 1 or a higher grade. It is, therefore, recommended that during an intake, the teacher receives information on the L1 language development of the child, and whether they like to read at home/are being read to. This can already give indications of what to expect regarding L2 development and what level of intervention might be needed.

4.3.2   Stimulating Reading, Both in L1 and L2

The best way to become proficient in a language is practice. So, the child should be encouraged to read books, watch movies and series, listen to songs, and engage in other activities in which they are confronted with the L2. However, because of linguistic transfer, reading in the L1 should certainly also be encouraged and supported. An important aspect here is motivation: being motivated to read and enjoying reading, play a significant role in advancing reading skills (Mol & Bus, 2011). Motivation comes from self-determination (Ryan & Deci, 2000). If a child can make choices, and be in control of their own learning process, intrinsic motivation will be higher. For example, the purpose of improving the second language, practical benefits, and intrinsic values play a role: why would you want to learn the new language? Experiencing progress and success contribute to reading motivation (Toste et al., 2020). According to De Burgh-Hirabe (2013), reading motivation is influenced more by reading materials and a student's attitude towards reading in the second language than by low reading skills or the sociocultural environment. Furthermore, the first two components can compensate for the latter two components. Some students may experience anxiety towards reading in their L2: this is often linked to how difficult they think the language is to read (Saito et al., 1999). In these cases, teachers can help students by first looking for ways to reduce their anxiety. To stimulate motivation, teachers may engage in a contest, for example setting a reading goal for a number of pages to read for the coming week, or providing a fun activity or reward when students have finished a book.

4.3.3 Developing L2 Lexical Quality

As is clear from the literature, a lower level of vocabulary is associated with lower reading comprehension. To stimulate L2 vocabulary, it is crucial to do this in context, to address lexical quality. But the teaching and learning of vocabulary can often be experienced as a boring activity, both by children and by the teacher. Using mind maps in the form of playful game-like activities (Yip & Kwan, 2006) may be one solution. These mind maps can help show the relationships between words and concepts. For example, words can be connected based on the theme (e.g., the zoo), associations (e.g., linking to students' own experiences), how words sound, or hierarchy (e.g., different kinds of animals that fall in the same category such as baby animals) (Drager et al., 2010; Mirman et al., 2017). In promoting vocabulary development, it can be relevant to pay attention not only to the meaning of a word, but also to its form, for example, how a word is pronounced and how it is spelled (Janssen et al., 2019). Other ways to teach vocabulary include repeating words in different contexts, using cooperative games to practice using the new words, and, where relevant, drawing attention to derived words (e.g., stabilize, destabilize, stabilizers, stabilization, etc.). Using specific methods repeatedly creates familiar routines that help students in their learning process. In all, it is very relevant to teach word meanings to children. As was the case in the previous principle, self- determination is key.

4.3.4 Teaching Specific L2 Reading Strategies

Being able to derive the meaning of an unknown word from the context is an important word learning strategy (Fukkink & de Glopper, 1998), and even more so for those reading in their L2, as they will encounter more unknown words. The strategy is not a specific L2 reading strategy, but it is of particular importance for L2 readers, and hence should be prioritized. Teachers could also help children learn to use morphological information to deduce the meaning of an unknown word via affixes and suffixes (McCutchen & Logan, 2011). For example, words ending with -ist may refer to a person who knows a lot about a certain subject or holds certain beliefs. In their review study on effective methods for language stimulation, Vanbuel and Van den Branden (2020) also included second language learners. They write that it is important to integrate different strategies and approaches in the classroom, such as direct instruction, summarizing, and explicit attention to vocabulary. It is important that students know why and when strategies are useful, and to prompt students to use them both during and after reading.

4.3.5 Using the L1 Proficiency

In some countries, multilingual students receive instruction in their L1 by law, as this is seen as a cultural right. However, the L1 can also be seen as a means to support L2 instruction as noted by Fung et al. (2003), who evidenced the benefit of using L1-assisted reciprocal teaching. Children may also activate prior knowledge, which is relevant for comprehension, by reading in the L1. When asking students if they know words about a certain subject, the teacher can ask students if they also know words in a different language, which may lead to a broader scope of words, and to new vocabulary learning. When explaining, for example, the past tense, students may grasp the concept more easily when they realize they already know (of) the concept in their L1. This does not mean that teachers should constantly refer to or use students' L1, but the use of, and respect for, L1 proficiency, may be a powerful way to enhance L2 reading comprehension. As described in Sect. 4.3.1, it may be helpful to ask parents about their child's L1 proficiency and development: this may give ideas about how to connect their L1 and their L2. If the child's L1 is also taught at school, the child's L1 teacher may have useful insights.

4.4 In summary

✓ Monitor students' reading development, especially for multilingual students, and pay attention to how students' reading comprehension skills develop over time and which areas need extra attention.

✓ Stimulate reading by encouraging and supporting students to read in all available languages.

✓ Develop students' second language lexical quality by teaching vocabulary in meaningful ways.

✓ When teaching reading strategies, include specific strategies for second language learning.

✓ Use first language proficiency to activate prior knowledge.

References

August, D. E., & Shanahan, T. E. (2006). *Developing literacy in second-language learners: Report of the National Literacy Panel on language-minority children and youth.* Lawrence Erlbaum Associates Publishers.

Burgess, S. R. (2011). Home literacy environments (HLEs) provided to very young children. *Early Child Development and Care, 181*(4), 445–462. https://doi.org/10.1080/03004430903450384

Burgoyne, K., Whiteley, H. E., & Hutchinson, J. M. (2013). The role of background knowledge in text comprehension for children learning English as an additional language. *Journal of Research in Reading, 36*(2), 132–148.

Cummins, J. (1979). Linguistic interdependence and the educational development of bilingual children. *Review of Educational Research, 49,* 222–251.

Cummins, J. (2001). HER classic reprint: Empowering minority students: A framework for intervention. *Harvard Educational Review, 71*(4), 649–676.

Davidse, N. J., de Jong, M. T., Bus, A. G., Huijbregts, S. C. J., & Swaab, H. (2011). Cognitive and environmental predictors of early literacy skills. *Reading and Writing: An Interdisciplinary Journal, 24*(4), 395–412.

De Burgh-Hirabe, R. (2013). A model of motivation for extensive reading in Japanese as a foreign language. *Reading in a Foreign Language, 25*(1), 72–93.

Drager, K. D. R., Finke, E. H., & Serpentine, E. C. (2010). Augmentative and alternative communication: An introduction. In J. S. Damico, N. Müller, & M. J. Ball (Eds.), *The handbook of language and speech disorders* (pp. 410–430). Blackwell Publishing Ltd. https://doi.org/10.1002/978144 4318975.ch18

Droop, M., & Verhoeven, L. (2003). Language proficiency and reading ability in first-and second-language learners. *Reading Research Quarterly, 38*(1), 78–103.

Fukkink, R. G., & de Glopper, K. (1998). Effects of instruction in deriving word meaning from context: A meta-analysis. *Review of Educational Research, 68*(4), 450–469.

Fung, I. Y., Wilkinson, I. A., & Moore, D. W. (2003). L1-assisted reciprocal teaching to improve ESL students' comprehension of English expository text. *Learning and Instruction, 13*(1), 1–31.

Genesee, F., Paradis, J., & Crago, M. B. (2004). *Dual language development and disorders: A handbook on bilingualism and second language learning,* Vol. 11. Paul H Brookes Publishing.

Janssen, C., Segers, E., McQueen, J. M., & Verhoeven, L. (2019). Comparing effects of instruction on word meaning and word form on early literacy abilities in kindergarten. *Early Education and Development, 30*(3), 375–399.

Lervåg, A., & Aukrust, V. G. (2010). Vocabulary knowledge is a critical determinant of the difference in reading comprehension growth between first and second language learners. *Journal of Child Psychology and Psychiatry, 51*(5), 612–620.

Mancilla-Martinez, J., & Lesaux, N. K. (2010). Predictors of reading comprehension for struggling readers: The case of Spanish-speaking language minority learners. *Journal of Educational Psychology, 102*(3), 701.

McCutchen, D., & Logan, B. (2011). Inside incidental word learning: Children's strategic use of morphological information to infer word meanings. *Reading Research Quarterly, 46*(4), 334–349.

Melby-Lervåg, M., & Lervåg, A. (2011). Cross-linguistic transfer of oral language, decoding, phonological awareness and reading comprehension: A meta-analysis of the correlational evidence. *Journal of Research in Reading, 34*(1), 114–135.

Melby-Lervåg, M., & Lervåg, A. (2014). Reading comprehension and its underlying components in second-language learners: A meta-analysis of studies comparing first- and second-language learners. *Psychological Bulletin, 140*(2), 409.

Mirman, D., Landrigan, J. F., & Britt, A. E. (2017). Taxonomic and thematic semantic systems. *Psychological Bulletin, 143*(5), 499–520. https://doi-org.ru.idm.oclc.org/10.1037/bul0000092

Mol, S. E., & Bus, A. G. (2011). To read or not to read: A meta-analysis of print exposure from infancy to early adulthood. *Psychological Bulletin, 137*(2), 267.

Proctor, C. P., Silverman, R. D., Harring, J. R., & Montecillo, C. (2012). The role of vocabulary depth in predicting reading comprehension among English monolingual and Spanish-English bilingual children in elementary school. *Reading and Writing: An Interdisciplinary Journal, 25,* 1635–1664. https://doi.org/10.1007/s11145-011-9336-5

Ryan, R. M., & Deci, E. L. (2000). Self-determination theory and the facilitation of intrinsic motivation, social development, and well-being. *American Psychologist, 55*(1), 68.

Saito, Y., Horwitz, E. K., & Garza, T. J. (1999). Foreign language reading anxiety. *Modern Language Journal, 83,* 202–218.

Schaars, M. M., Segers, E., & Verhoeven, L. (2019). Cognitive and linguistic precursors of early first and second language reading development. *Learning and Individual Differences, 72*, 1–14.

Toste, J. R., Didion, L., Peng, P., Filderman, M. J., & McClelland, A. M. (2020). A meta- analytic review of the relations between motivation and reading achievement for K–12 students. *Review of Educational Research, 90*(3), 420–456.

Van den Bosch, L. J., Segers, E., & Verhoeven, L. (2019). The role of linguistic diversity in the prediction of early reading comprehension: A quantile regression approach. *Scientific Studies of Reading, 23*(3), 203–219.

Van den Bosch, L. J., Segers, E., & Verhoeven, L. (2020). First and second language vocabulary affect early second language reading comprehension development. *Journal of Research in Reading, 43*(3), 290–308.

Vanbuel, M., & Van den Branden, K. (2020). Promoting primary school pupils' language achievement: Investigating the impact of school-based language policies. *School Effectiveness and School Improvement, 1–23.* https://doi.org/10.1080/09243453.2020.1812675

Verhoeven, L., & Van Leeuwe, J. (2012). The simple view of second language reading throughout the primary grades. *Reading and Writing, 25*, 1805–1818.

Yip, F. W., & Kwan, A. C. (2006). Online vocabulary games as a tool for teaching and learning English vocabulary. *Educational Media International, 43*(3), 233–249.

Chapter 5
Good Practices in Teaching Reading Comprehension from Five PIRLS Countries

Inspiring Examples of Reading Education for Multilingual Students

Abstract In the final chapter of this book, good practices from five participating PIRLS countries are highlighted. In these five countries from various parts of the world, multilingual students do relatively well on the PIRLS achievement test. One or two schools from each country present how their teachers work on reading comprehension, specifically for multilingual students. The descriptions of the schools' education in reading comprehension are supplemented with practical tips and example lessons. These practical suggestions and ideas can inspire teachers all over the world to strengthen their own lessons in reading comprehension.

Keywords Reading comprehension · Good practices · PIRLS countries · Multilingual students

5.1 Introduction

In this chapter, we provide a glimpse into reading education in seven schools across five PIRLS countries. These schools proudly share their experiences and advice regarding reading education, specifically for students with a home language that is different to the language of instruction. With these stories, they hope to inspire teachers all over the world and contribute ideas for organizing reading education in their own classrooms.

We have selected five PIRLS countries from various parts of the world, where multilingual students perform relatively well on the PIRLS achievement test. In these countries, there is a moderately small difference in performance on the PIRLS achievement test between multilingual students and monolingual students. One or two schools from each country present how their teachers work on reading comprehension, specifically with multilingual students. The description of the school's education in reading comprehension is supplemented with example lessons. These good practices can inspire teachers all over the world to strengthen their own lessons. For more information about the countries and their educational systems, reading curricula in the primary grades, and overall policies related to reading instruction, see the online PIRLS encyclopedia (Mullis et al., 2017). A more extensive version

© The Author(s) 2022   89
M. Bruggink et al., *Putting PIRLS to Use in Classrooms Across the Globe*, IEA Research for Educators 1, https://doi.org/10.1007/978-3-030-95266-2_5

of this chapter can be found on the IEA website—https://www.iea.nl/putting-pirls-to-use/chapter-5.

Schools that contributed to this chapter are:

- Colegio Técnico Profesional los Acacios in Chile
- Donghe Elementary School in Chinese Taipei
- Chesterton Primary School in England
- Elmhurst Primary School in England
- Bolnisi Municipality Vill Darbazi Public School in Georgia
- Public school #2 of Akhalkaki in Georgia
- Isaac Peral Primary School in Spain

5.2 Good Practices from Chile

Colegio Técnico Profesional los Acacios

ABOUT COLEGIO TÉCNICO PROFESIONAL LOS ACACIOS

Colegio Técnico Profesional los Acacios is an educational institution located in the south-central zone of Chile, in the city of Concepción, specifically in the Biobío region. This school provides primary and secondary education for children and youth in the local area.

Teacher Laura Marianjel Discusses Teaching Reading Comprehension at Colegio Técnico Profesional los Acacios

5.2.1 Integrating Reading Comprehension with Other Subjects

In higher grades, we work with the daily activity of doing "daily comments." These are based on a set of short readings, which are connected to other subjects. For example, if in mathematics the students are working with measurements, then we might work with recipes. We read different recipes, their ingredients, and their respective measurements in grams and kilograms. Another example is, if they are learning about countries of America and their typical foods in history, in the reading classes we will work with a recipe for a typical meal from Venezuela or Brazil (in my case because I have students of those nationalities). A passage or text is read out loud every morning in front of the class, and boys and girls prepare a brief written comment. The text is analyzed, promoting the acquisition of new vocabulary, association with their own environment, interaction of experiences, etc.

5.2.2 Beyond Just Reading: Storytelling and Home Activities

In the beginning, the teacher guides reading. We implement an activity called "modeled reading" (*lectura modelada*), where the teacher reads out loud in front of the whole class. Then, one student will begin to read for the others. This is done using books with illustrations, but also by being storytellers. In this activity, the teacher can wear a distinctive costume or hat (e.g., a crown or a witch's hat) to tell a story, or a guardian is invited to the classroom to dramatize a story.

Reading and comprehension are then encouraged using instructional texts that involve concrete materials, where students show their understanding by delivering a product such as an origami or drawing.

To work on vocabulary with students who speak a language other than Spanish, the same literacy process is used. They will learn more words by associating them with images and with examples about meaningful contexts in which they occur. To use the same example of the recipe, grade 2 students had to write a recipe that is usually made in their home, one they had made themselves, or a recipe that they like. With great enthusiasm, the children wrote recipes, but they also experienced them by cooking the recipes themselves and sharing photos and videos. This was particularly significant because cooking was their own idea: they wanted to go beyond simply completing or submitting the homework.

5.2.3 Acting Out a Story: A Classroom Example

One of the objectives of the reading class is for students to learn to demonstrate understanding of texts by answering explicit and implicit questions about them. Implicit questions involve a more complex skill for some students. A strategy that helps students to understand what is explicit and what is implicit, is through brief performances with narrations, improvised during the lesson by the teacher, using concepts or vocabulary from the texts read. This type of performance consists of the following:

The teacher walks around the room talking about what a child was doing one afternoon at home: "I'm going to look out the window to see if my dad arrives. I have to have my room completely tidied up before he gets home, because he can get angry if he sees a lot of clutter in my room." After that, the students are asked about what the character did and narrated, indicating that this corresponds to the explicit information in the text (everything they heard and saw). Then, the students answer an implicit question, for example: How does the character feel prior to the arrival of the dad?

DIDACTIC PRINCIPLES AT COLEGIO TÉCNICO PROFESIONAL LOS ACACIOS

At Colegio Técnico Profesional los Acacios teachers activate students' prior knowledge before reading a text. The different type of texts they select for their students are meaningful and motivate students to read. Subjects like mathematics are integrated with reading. By dramatizing, teachers visualize stories to enhance comprehension. For multilingual students, the meaning of words are clarified and teachers encourage students to talk about their native country and culture.

5.3   Good Practices from Chinese Taipei

Donghe Elementary School

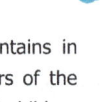

ABOUT DONGHE ELEMENTARY SCHOOL

Donghe Elementary School is a small school in the mountains in the west part of the country. The school includes speakers of the SaySiyat, Atayal, and Hakka languages, and new immigrant children who speak other languages.

Teachers Chin-Chu Kao, Meng-Chu Pan, Ting-Xi Zhu, Chia-Chia Hsu, and Zhi-Liang Yeh Discuss Teaching Reading Comprehension at Donghe Elementary School

5.3.1   Sharing a Multilingual Environment

The school includes speakers of SaySiyat, Atayal, and Hakka, as well as immigrant children who speak other languages. In addition to the curriculum formulated by the

Ministry of Education, the school also provides opportunities for the students to know and respect each other's culture. The school's curriculum is a reading program based on multilingualism. Teaching is mainly done in the SaySiyat language (one of the indigenous languages in Taiwan), supplemented by other languages, such as Chinese and Atayal. Teachers integrate the texts with multicultural topics to encourage the students to have a good learning atmosphere and positive interactions with each other.

Grade 1 and 2 students have been exposed to the immersion learning environment of the SaySiyat language when they were in kindergarten. Therefore, they usually speak some simple words of SaySiyat at school. Teachers have conversations with the students using some simple SaySiyat and encourage the students to answer in SaySiyat. The school produces many picture books in the SaySiyat language. Students who are not familiar with the spelling of SaySiyat language might read slowly, or even have difficulty in reading. Hence, teachers have the students practice pronunciation first, which helps construct the foundation of reading. Then, teachers read the picture books with the students, and guide them to observe and learn from the picture books. There are a lot of websites related to ethnic languages, such as ethnic language E paradise (族語E樂園). There are abundant resources for the students on these websites, such as animated films, picture books, and so on. We hope that the students can learn their ethnic languages through reading. To speak more, the students sometimes practice using their ethnic languages to tell stories to their classmates during the morning meeting at school. If the teachers in other fields are from SaySiyat, they will give instructions in class, and have conversations with the students using some SaySiyat language in order to support them in getting used to bilingual circumstances. If English teachers also teach in other fields such as social studies, they will have conversations with the students by using some English words to make them familiar with English. We take the students with a different language and cultural background into account in our reading education. We combine teachers' language specialty with the resources on the websites to let the students learn and comprehend the texts in different fields by using multiple languages and drawing on multiple cultures.

5.3.2 Growing in Reading Comprehension Through Interaction and Motivation

For grade 1 and 2 students, it is suggested that teachers let the students look at the pictures first, and then interact with them by asking questions, and finally talk about the texts. The students discuss the texts, and practice asking and answering questions for reading comprehension. The students learn from each other by expressing their opinions. It is also recommended that the students practice their thinking ability by reading more picture books and discussing them with their peers. Teachers must also know how to support the students' preference for reading. For example, grade 1 and 2 students especially like to watch animated picture books. As a result, they express their ideas eagerly when having discussions. Teachers speaking in SaySiyat or English use complete sentences to ask questions or have conversations with the students. When they cannot understand the whole sentence, they try to guess the meanings from the context or keywords. That helps them not only to acquire ethnic languages, but also to apply the strategies of reading comprehension. It is suggested that teachers create interesting situations, interact with the students in lively dialogues, and have them say some simple sentences. The students will strengthen their learning motivation and use the language they learned when they can say some sentences. It is also recommended that teachers provide the students with multiple text types, including texts in different languages. Students are also encouraged to apply self-learning strategies as they comprehend texts in different languages. Furthermore, teachers teach the students how to evaluate the source of online texts and news, as well as to select what they need from the broad online knowledge to help themselves learn.

DIDACTIC PRINCIPLES AT DONGHE ELEMENTARY SCHOOL

The didactic principles integrated at Donghe Elementary School include students' interactions about texts through cooperative group work, and the integration of reading with other subjects. The use of various strategies (such as predicting, monitoring comprehension, questioning, and summarizing) and how to apply these in different languages is implemented in the lessons. The school takes students with different language and cultural backgrounds into account. Teachers select texts with multicultural issues and encourage discussion to ensure respect for each other's culture.

5.4   Good Practices from England

Chesterton Primary School

> **ABOUT CHESTERTON PRIMARY SCHOOL**
>
> Chesterton Primary School is a larger than average state-funded school situated in an area of high deprivation in South West London. The percentage of pupils who speak English as an additional language is in the top 20% of all schools nationally. More than half of the parents have limited spoken and written English and the percentage of pupils from ethnic minority backgrounds is 87%. Chesterton Primary School is a Teaching School, Mathematics Hub, English Hub, and an Early Years Hub which means that it supports other state-funded schools in London to improve their provision and outcomes across the curriculum.

Deputy Head Victoria Linke Discusses Teaching Reading Comprehension at Chesterton Primary School

5.4.1   Reading in a Multilingual Environment

At Chesterton, all staff have received vocabulary development training, and we make sure that oracy is an ongoing focus of all curriculum areas. Every lesson starts with 10 min of vocabulary time, and the children are introduced to a new word each day. These words are displayed on the classroom wall and the children are encouraged to use them in their daily conversation and writing. We have a strong focus on the development of language and language skills for our children because we know that speaking and listening are crucial skills for reading and writing in all subjects. Where language could present a potential barrier, we ensure there are additional visuals in place and sentence stems to support the children. We promote the use of dual language books through our school library, where the children can freely select a book in multiple languages to share with their families at home. In addition, we use the school website as an alternative resource for families, where they can access online videos of our school staff reading books in English and a range of other languages.

5.4.2   *Frederick Douglass: An Example of Reading Material that Connects to Students' Experiences*

In grade 6 (10–11-year-olds), the children learned about apartheid as their overarching topic for the term. In our reading lessons, they each had a copy of Fredrick Douglass' biography. Frederick Douglass, an escaped slave who became a prominent activist, author, and public speaker, was a leader in the abolitionist movement, which sought to end the practice of slavery, before and during the United States Civil War. This topic and book were selected because it is a culturally significant period in world history, exposing many issues that our children at Chesterton can relate to and/or have a connection with. The teacher began by explaining why she had chosen this book and provided information about the author and other books that the author had written. This process is important because the teacher can model the selection process and generate enthusiasm to engage the class with the book. The class then began to disentangle the key features and purpose of a non-fiction text, so all children could access the text. The next part of the lesson focused on reading with fluency and, after an initial discussion around key vocabulary, the children took it in turns to read with a partner. This process was modeled to the children beforehand, so there was a clear expectation about how to support each other. Once the children had the opportunity to read the set pages, the teacher posed a series of questions relating to retrieval and inference, where the answers were discussed in small groups and then shared as a class. As the children were so engaged in this reading material and subsequent book talk, several of them chose to go to the library after school to select other books about Black History to take home and share with their families.

DIDACTIC PRINCIPLES AT CHESTERTON PRIMARY SCHOOL

At Chesterton Primary School, the focus for young children is mainly on decoding. For every class, rich, authentic reading materials are selected, and students talk about these reading materials. Teachers model how students can increase text comprehension. They monitor the students' level of reading comprehension and use this information in follow-up lessons. A lot of extra attention is paid to learning new words, which are made visible in the classroom. The home language of students is embraced; not only is reading in English encouraged, but also reading in the home language(s).

Elmhurst Primary School

> **ABOUT ELMHURST PRIMARY SCHOOL**
>
> Elmhurst Primary School is a large, four form primary school in Newham, East London. Newham is one of the most deprived London boroughs. Over 95% of the pupils speak languages other than English at home. The school is a national English and Mathematics Hub and, as such, supports other schools in the area with their Mathematics and English provision.

Teacher Katharine Young Discusses Teaching Reading Comprehension at Elmhurst Primary School

5.4.3 Expanding Vocabulary as the First Step for Multilingual Students

At Elmhurst, the overwhelming majority of our pupils speak languages other than English at home. This means that everything that we do at school has the needs of multilingual students at its heart.

Key new vocabulary is introduced carefully in each lesson before pupils are exposed to it through reading, both in KS1 and KS2. In KS2, strategies for clarifying the meaning of words are taught explicitly, and new words are explored in depth to ensure a full understanding of a word, especially those which can have multiple meanings. New vocabulary is identified in planning and taught explicitly in all subjects. We never assume prior knowledge of subject specific vocabulary, as our pupils are unlikely to have come across these words in the past. Grammar is taught explicitly to ensure that pupils know how to construct sentences that are grammatically correct in English. A key focus for us is the correct use of prepositions and verbs.

We also have a significant number of new admissions each year for whom English is a totally new language. For those pupils who arrive from overseas during KS1, pupils join the group most suitable for their stage of learning in phonics. For those who arrive during KS2, we usually provide small-group teaching with other pupils in a similar position to allow them to focus on learning to decode and expanding their vocabulary rapidly, with the aim that they are able to join the main teaching class within two years of arrival in the school.

We do not generally provide reading activities in home languages for pupils as part of our normal classroom provision, although for the more common community languages (e.g., Gujarati, Arabic, Bengali, Urdu) we have after-school clubs which are run by native speakers.

5.4.4 "The Malfeasance": An Example of Modeling a Strategy for Reading Comprehension

In order to develop both clarifying and comprehension monitoring, I taught a lesson to a grade 6 group which focused on the fairly challenging poem "The Malfeasance," by Alan Bold. I asked the pupils to first predict what the poem might be about, based only on the title. Pupils were then asked to read the text and explain what it was about. They were unable to do this as they had not monitored their own understanding. They were then asked to annotate the poem with their thoughts and questions. This was modeled for the first two stanzas. Pupils then continued to annotate the rest of the poem.

After this was complete, pupils were asked again to explain what the poem was about and to answer some questions about it. All pupils demonstrated a much better understanding of the text as they had been taught the strategy of text marking. Some pupils were also able to identify the moral of the poem.

DIDACTIC PRINCIPLES AT ELMHURST PRIMARY SCHOOL

At Elmhurst Primary School, several didactic principles are being integrated. In Key Stage 1, teachers focus mainly on decoding words. This is important because English is such an opaque language (see Chapter 1). Reading strategies like clarifying, summarizing, predicting, questioning, and monitoring understanding are taught explicitly to the older students. There is interaction about texts in small groups, and reading and writing are integrated very naturally. In addition, teachers at Elmhurst Primary School spend time stimulating reading for pleasure. Given the large number of multilingual students at the school, there is also a lot of focus on learning the meaning of new words.

5.5   Good Practices from Georgia

Bolnisi Municipality Vill Darbazi Public school

> **ABOUT BOLNISI MUNICIPALITY VILL DARBAZI PUBLIC SCHOOL**
>
> Bolnisi Municipality Vill Darbazi Public school is located in the mountainous village of Darbazi in East Georgia, in the Kvemo Kartli Region. Bolnisi Municipality is mainly populated with ethnically Georgian and Azerbaijani families, but in Darbazi the majority of the population is ethnically Azerbaijani. The school is Azerbaijani, therefore the primary language of teaching is Azerbaijani. Georgian, the state language of the country, is taught as a second language for five academic hours per week.

Teacher Sevda (Khalilova) Muzashvili Discusses Teaching Reading Comprehension at Bolnisi Municipality Vill Darbazi Public school

5.5.1   Teaching Georgian at the School

Georgian, the state language, is taught from grade 1 in minority schools in Georgia. At the elementary level, we start with teaching words using illustrations in Georgian language lessons. A student hears names of objects and is expected to logically match words with relevant pictures. These pictures are usually united under certain themes, for instance: "our yard," "my family," "school," "farm," etc. We assist students to memorize these words so that they can later use them to compose short sentences.

Repetition of the same thing helps students to memorize words better. Students enjoy asking each other questions, and teachers try to transform this interaction into games. For example, students impersonate different animals and ask each other relevant questions. They like this activity and gain affection towards learning through games. Such entertaining activities help students to remember many words. No less important is the application of proper gesturing when explaining words related to feelings and emotions. Those words that are difficult to express through illustrations, such as caressing, irritation, empathy, etc., are usually explained through gestures and body language. This helps students to enrich their vocabulary, which also facilitates acquiring the basic knowledge and skills fundamental to reading comprehension.

For the elementary grades (1–6) we select short texts, based on the words students have already learned. At this stage, it is necessary to start introducing new words as well. For homework, students are asked to make an illustration of a new word in a vocabulary workbook to facilitate better memorization of this word. Then they show their classmates their picture and describe it. The class is divided into groups of five students, where each group is given a separate word to draw. This method allows students to memorize several new words in a day if they rotate, so each group has to illustrate, for instance, five words. Afterwards, we put students' illustrations on the walls. Finally, we ask students to make up new stories and invent new characters using several illustrated words. Students then encounter these newly learned words in a different context with new characters. We select texts that are well-adapted to the demands of a particular classroom. Namely, texts are selected based on the analysis of classroom needs, taking into consideration the readiness of students and the level they are at. The new text is read by the teacher. I read with pauses, simultaneously observing if students are listening with attention. While reading, I try to convey the content of the text with relevant emotions. Thus, the teacher assesses students' ability to comprehend, asking questions such as: What do you think will happen next? How will the events unfold? How would you end the text? What would you do if you were in his place?

5.5.2   Integrating Reading and Writing in the Context of Natural Science

In our school, the subject of natural sciences has been taught in the state language for two years. Georgian language teachers and natural science teachers work together on the thematic texts that have been compiled in advance for the students. The Georgian language teacher teaches new words, instructing how to pronounce and write them correctly, use them accordingly in a sentence, and comply with grammar rules. We work together on the lexical definitions. Moreover, we also use short video stories to make learning about the subject interesting and fun. Afterwards, we ask students to write short texts based on the story shown before.

5.5.3   Texts for Different Levels

Our texts are divided into levels: low, medium, and high. Each level becomes more complicated as new, more extensive and compound sentences are added. Here we are allowed to apply the differentiated approach: every student requires an individual approach, and therefore books of different levels are used to guide us. Grade 1 students have access to special software enriched with relevant texts and assignments that have been pre-recorded on the laptops provided to them by the state. These resources are actively used both in the classroom and for homework. The texts used for upper grades are completely different from those used for the primary level.

Texts selected for older students are more profound. A properly selected teaching approach, equal, with respectful attitudes towards the students, and the ability to listen and tolerate different opinions, creates respectful interaction between students and teachers, and simultaneously increases motivation to learn. Therefore, the student is no longer focused on summative, but on formative assessment, and becomes your ally in learning. The student becomes motivated and wants to learn, and this is an ultimate goal of every teacher. This is why I try to select a text that ignites students' desire for analysis.

DIDACTIC PRINCIPLES AT BOLNISI MUNICIPALITY VILL DARBAZI PUBLIC SCHOOL

At Bolnisi Municipality Vill Darbazi Public school, teachers focus on vocabulary for the youngest students. This is done in a playful way, explaining the meaning of words in various ways. The school has integrated reading and writing in the context of natural science. Teachers differentiate between students by using texts that are appropriate for the individual student. Formative assessment is used to actively involve students in their learning process.

Public school #2

ABOUT PUBLIC SCHOOL #2 IN AKHALKAKI

Akhalkalaki is a small town in the Samtskhe-Javakheti region, in the south of Georgia. The majority of the population of the town is ethnically Armenian. The school's primary language of teaching is Russian, with Georgian, the state language, being taught as a second language quite intensively (five academic hours a week, i.e., one hour every day), and Armenian, a native language of the population, being taught as a foreign language.

Teacher Shorena Tetvadze Discusses Teaching Reading Comprehension at the Public School #2 in Akhalkaki

5.5.4 Enriching Reading Lessons to Increase Reading Motivation

To make the learning process fun for students, lessons should be enriched with interesting and interactive methods. The more multifaceted and versatile the lesson, the more interest and responsibility are demonstrated by students towards learning. In this regard, increasing student motivation depends on the teachers. It is effective and productive to use the method "learning through playing and doing." When planning the lesson and activities, teachers take into consideration students' abilities, interests, and the fact that each student requires a differentiated approach. Consequently, we try to create an environment where all students are equally involved in the learning process. To achieve better results, both the teacher and the student must be equipped with a variety of resources that will be effectively and efficiently used in the teaching and learning process. Bringing books to life by introducing theatrical or on-screen adaptations of the text is an integral part of becoming a good reader. The application of role-play in the lesson process is no longer a novelty. This method, above all, helps to improve the ability to read thoughtfully and increases the motivation to read. Teachers and parents should acknowledge the fact that reading is fun and not a boring necessity. Teachers should ignite students' motivation to read, by suggesting appropriate texts, organizing literary evenings in informal settings, and offering various encouragements, which will consequently transform students into good readers. We have created a suitable environment for refined and cultured readers in our school: a library, a readers' club, active participation of parents, frequent visits by interesting persons, book discussions with students, performances, debates, and rewarding students when they improve their reading to increase motivation.

5.5.5 "Penguin Pepe": An Example Reading Lesson

This lesson was planned for different age groups at the primary level. The objective was that students would be able to read a short text, comprehend it, express their attitude, make assumptions about the story, and write a simple text.

Before reading: To motivate students and introduce the topic of the lesson, I showed students excerpts from a cartoon about a penguin. I then asked the following questions: "What was the film about? Do you know anything about it?" Then I asked them to explain why I showed this excerpt and what our lesson would be about. I then showed students the auxiliary learning material, a book about "Penguin Pepe." We contemplated the illustration on the book cover, and I informed students that we would be reading and discussing a text about a penguin. I introduced the topic and the purpose of the lesson to the students and provided information about reading strategies they would have to work with during the lesson.

During the reading: The second phase of reading aims to equip students with new knowledge and skills through actively working with the text. I started reading the text by reading the first part aloud. The text was then read by students through the application of different reading strategies, including continuous, pointed reading, reading with pauses, etc. During the reading process, through the application of different methods—thinking aloud, asking questions, making assumptions—I made sure that the students understood the text they had read. After completing the reading, we listened to an audio recording of the same text, which refreshed students' memories and allowed them to further clarify the details and events given in the text. Afterwards, we went back to the text again, guiding students to understand the text better by asking additional questions. Students further explored the text's details and were asked to fill in a table about the characteristics of the three animals which appear in the story.

After reading: The goal of the third phase is to guide students to use their knowledge and skills to discuss key issues, summarize, answer questions, or make an interesting creative product. Accordingly, after reading and processing the text, I asked the students to help the penguin to complete the sentence, "The elephant is…" and later drew a relevant illustration for it.

Evaluation: At the end of the lesson, the students evaluated the lesson, explored and discussed which activity they liked the most, whether they were active, whether their expectations were met, and which topic they would like to learn more about in the future. I used "the A-B-C review" to evaluate the students: students were asked to find a word from the text, beginning with the indicated letter, and write down what they had learned about it.

DIDACTIC PRINCIPLES AT PUBLIC SCHOOL #2 IN AKHALKAKI

At Public school #2 in Akhalkaki, reading is fully integrated into the curriculum of other lessons. Teachers use different reading strategies, like visualizing, predicting, asking questions, and summarizing, to enhance text comprehension. Students are taught to critically analyze texts. Therefore, interaction and discussion about the content of the text takes place. Teachers focus on increasing student motivation to read by using interesting and interactive methods and creating a rich reading environment.

5.6   Good Practices from Spain

Isaac Peral primary school

> **ABOUT ISAAC PERAL PRIMARY SCHOOL**
>
> Isaac Peral Primary School is located in the northeast region of Spain, on the outskirts of Barcelona, in the town of Terrassa. Being a local school, it only has one single class per course, offering neighborhood schooling for about 230 children aged 3 to 12 years old. The neighborhood's inhabitants are mainly working class, and during the past decades the number of immigrants has increased enormously, with many from Africa and Latin America. So, most of our students have either Arabic or Spanish as their mother tongue. The first language of the school is Catalan, then Castilian Spanish and English as a foreign language.

Teachers Imma Puig, Rosa Raya, Susana González and M. Roser Garcia Discuss Teaching Reading Comprehension at the Isaac Peral Primary School

5.6.1   Students with Different Language Backgrounds

First, it is important to differentiate students who come from a lower socioeconomic background or with limited cultural experiences from those who come from backgrounds of medium and higher socioeconomic status or with rich cultural experiences. The first group are usually students with knowledge of a single language, which is usually different from the language used at the school. This makes it more difficult for them to acquire other languages. In our school, they have to learn Catalan, Spanish, and English simultaneously. Students in the second group tend to have enhanced stimuli in their environment. For this reason, it is not too difficult for them to acquire a new language.

In both cases, we begin by working with them on basic vocabulary through individualized lessons or in "reception classrooms" during language classes. Teachers make a list of specific vocabulary to work on, and they learn most of the vocabulary through projects that they work on in the regular classrooms. Several digital materials are also used, as well as visual references (which are either our own or taken from the internet).

We do not work on specific texts in the language of the student. Although our school is sensitive to other languages, we only work in texts written in Catalan,

Spanish, or English. In order to make everyone feel integrated and aware of diversity, we encourage students to share vocabulary in their own languages during day-to-day life in the classroom. Sometimes there are also activities organized for the families of these students to share idioms and vocabulary that is characteristic of their place of origin. In cases in which families do not speak any of the languages that we work in at the school, we ask for someone to collaborate as a translator.

5.6.2 An Example of Using "Visualizing" in the Text "The Never-Ending Story"

5.6.2.1 Before Reading

I guide the students through the following stages:

- Connection: Today I will read you a fantastic story, but you have to close your eyes while you listen to it. What you will have to do is imagine where the characters are, how they are, and what the scenery is like.
- Modelling: I have also been imagining things while I was reading. I was thinking: "How could I imagine this forest, and the trees…? How can I imagine the luminous sphere if it is a fire but there is a figure inside that is neither a man nor a woman…?" (I would be thinking out loud so the students could ask themselves the same questions that I was asking myself. Later on, with the help of the students in the classroom, I would draw what we have visualized together on the blackboard.)
- Active participation: You will now read the second excerpt in pairs and you will have to imagine how the next scene will be. Ask each other questions; you can talk to classmates behind you and in front of you to expand your vision of the scene. Afterwards, you will draw what you have seen and imagined from the reading together.
- Link: Finally, you will read the next excerpt and do what we have done before all together and in pairs, now individually. If there is any word in the text that you do not understand we can all talk about it to make its interpretation easier. Go for it, your drawings will be fantastic. You have to think that no one will do a bad job because what is important here is your imagination, how you are visualizing what you are reading.

5.6.2.2 During the Reading

The students will read the text a second time and will then write down everything that can help them later when they have to draw: words, expressions, descriptions, etc. They can still ask questions to clear up any uncertainty about the vocabulary. I will give a sheet of paper to each one of them, so that they can start sketching what they are seeing and start building the scene.

5.6.2.3 After Reading

Finally, once the drawings are done, the students will show them to everyone in the classroom. Together we will comment on the differences between the drawing that they are viewing and their own. Every student, when showing their drawing, has to explain what strategy they followed. How did they imagine it, what things in the text helped them draw it in this way and not another, etc.? In this session it is important that everyone can explain what they have visualized and how they drew it.

The fact that the texts are in two different languages, Castilian and Catalan, should not be a problem. It is done on purpose because we also work with this strategy when it is time to work on writing skills, which we do in both languages.

DIDACTIC PRINCIPLES AT ISAAC PERAL PRIMARY SCHOOL

At Isaac Peral Primary School, teachers actively stimulate reading for pleasure. They motivate their students in various ways. One way is providing meaningful texts that are related to the students' world. Teachers give instructions about the use of reading strategies and word-learning strategies. Teachers monitor students' progress in reading comprehension and differentiate by giving extra instruction in vocabulary. The home language of the students is recognized in the daily lessons.

Reference

Mullis, I. V. S., Martin, M. O., Goh, S., & Prendergast, C. (Eds.). (2017). *PIRLS 2016 encyclopedia: Education policy and curriculum in reading*. Boston College, TIMSS & PIRLS International Study Center. http://timssandpirls.bc.edu/pirls2016/encyclopedia/

Glossary

Anaphoric relations Relations between linguistic expressions, where the interpretation of one linguistic expression (the anaphor) relies on the interpretation of another linguistic expression (the antecedent).

Comprehension strategies/ Reading Strategies Strategies that readers can use to support, monitor, and restore their understanding of the text.

Cognitive comprehension strategies help the reader to understand what they have read by performing activities before, during, or after reading.

Metacognitive comprehension strategies refer to activities to plan, monitor, and evaluate the reading process.

Decoding The process of converting strings of letters into their corresponding sounds.

Didactic The way in which teachers teach and help develop knowledge, skills, and attitudes.

Evidence-based Based on scientific insights.

Grapheme A letter or group of letters that represent(s) a sound (phoneme).

L1 First language.

L2 Second language.

Lexical quality How well a word (the written form, the pronunciation of the word, and its meaning) is known.

Linguistic transfer Process where knowledge of one language influences the learning of a second language.

Mental lexicon Place in long-term memory where knowledge about words is stored.

Modeling The process of making thoughts audible by saying what one is thinking while performing an action.

Multilingual Refers to the ability to express yourself and function in multiple languages.

Opaque language A language in which the consistency between written letters and sounds is low and single letters can correspond to more than one sound.

Organizer A tool to display the content of (parts of) the text in a graphical, structured way.

Orthography Writing/ written form of a word.

© International Association for the Evaluation of Educational Achievement (IEA) 2022   109
M. Bruggink et al., *Putting PIRLS to Use in Classrooms Across the Globe*, IEA Research for Educators 1, https://doi.org/10.1007/978-3-030-95266-2

Phoneme The smallest unit of a sound within a word.

Phonology Sounding/ spoken form of a word.

Proposition Semantic units, usually consisting of a relational term (predicate) and one or more arguments indicating semantic roles like agent, object, and goal. A proposition is considered the basic element of meaning.

Reading approach The way in which a reader reads a text.

Reading comprehension The ability to construct meaning from written texts.

Reading purpose The reason why a reader reads a text.

Semantics Meaning/ meaning of a word.

Situation model Integrates information explicitly stated in the text and relevant background knowledge.

Surface structure Consists of the words in the text and the ideas that these words represent.

Textbase Represents information explicitly stated in the text.

Transparant language A language in which the consistency between written letters and sounds is high and single letters generally correspond to a single sound, making it easy to convert a string of letters into a word.

Word identification The ability to identify words. Word identification starts with decoding a word, followed by retrieving information about the meaning of the word from long-term memory.

Word-to-text integration The ability to integrate the individual word meanings into the mental model of the text.

The manufacturer's authorised representative in the EU is Springer
Nature Customer Service Centre GmbH, Europaplatz 3, 69115 Heidelberg,
Germany. If you have any concerns regarding our products, please
contact ProductSafety@springernature.com

Printed and bound by CPI Group (UK) Ltd, Croydon, CR0 4YY
29/04/2026
02099522-0008